EXPERIENCING INTERNATIONAL BUSINESS AND MANAGEMENT

EXERCISES, PROJECTS, AND CASES

BETTY JANE PUNNETT

M.E.Sharpe
Armonk, New York
London, England

Library of Congress Cataloging-in-Publication Data

Punnett, Betty Jane.
    Experiencing international business and management: exercises, projects, and cases / by Betty Jane Punnett.
        p. cm.
    ISBN 0-7656-1515-0 (pbk.: alk. paper)
    1. International business enterprises—Management—Problems, exercises, etc. I. Title.

HD62.4.P86 2005
658′.049—dc22   2004017169

Printed in the United States of America

The paper used in this publication meets the minimum requirements of
American National Standard for Information Sciences
Permanence of Paper for Printed Library Materials,
ANSI Z 39.48-1984.

∞

MV (p)   10   9   8   7   6   5   4   3   2   1

Contents

Projects

Case Studies

List of Exhibits

Preface and Introduction to Experiential Learning

This book is intended to be a companion to any international business or international management text. It is especially intended as a supplement to Betty Jane Punnett's *International Perspectives on Organizational Behavior and Human Resources Management*, published by M.E. Sharpe (2004). Any instructor who wants to internationalize a business or management course will also find these exercises and projects an effective way of doing so.

International aspects of management are being integrated into university curricula throughout the United States and Canada, as well as in other countries. More than a decade ago, the American Association of Collegiate Schools of Business (AACSB) formally recognized the need for a greater international focus at the university level. The need for internationalization of the business curricula has grown even greater in the twenty-first century, and academic institutions are actively pursuing an increased international emphasis.

Many teaching approaches can be effective in pursuing this emphasis, including lectures, readings, library research, field research, case studies, and various types of simulations and exercises. Some teaching approaches focus on the study of theories and concepts; others focus on the real world and how theories and concepts apply in practice. Many instructors incorporate a blend of approaches into their classes.

This book presents a number of experiential exercises and projects for use in class and as homework. They illustrate some of the complexities of international management decisions and may be used in combination with the other teaching methods mentioned here. They have been designed to be fun, yet realistic; and students find that these exercises add an interesting and enjoyable dimension to class.

Introduction to Experiential Learning

Experiential learning broadly refers to learning that occurs from experience. If you cross the street without looking and get hit by a car, and if you learn from the experience to look both ways before crossing, then you have encountered experiential learning. Much of our learning is experiential, and we engage in experiential learning every day. In a classroom setting we attempt to achieve the same learning through the use of exercises that simulate a portion of the real world; we ask students to pretend the situation is real and make decisions in that context.

The overall learning process has been described in terms of four modes—concrete experience, reflective observation, abstract conceptualization, and active experimentation (see Kolb 1984, for a detailed discussion of these learning styles). People use all four of these styles, but different individuals may emphasize one or another and learn more effectively through that approach. Effective teaching incorporates opportunities to use all four learning styles. The most difficult to incorporate into the traditional classroom is *concrete experience*; the aim of the exercises and projects presented here is to provide an opportunity for some concrete experiences in the classroom.

Benefits of Experiential Learning

The exercises and projects in this text are intended to increase variety and interest in the classroom, while providing an effective learning environment. Proponents of experiential learning believe that:

- Learning is intensified when the process is interesting and fun.
- Learning generates involvement and interest when it provides active experience of concepts.
- Learning is effective when it is an active process rather than a passive one.
- Learning is most effective when thought, action, and feedback are integrated.
- Learning that involves two-way communication is most effective.
- Learning is enduring when it is problem-centered.

These exercises and projects are designed to take advantage of these benefits. They have been tested with student groups to ensure that students will find them interesting and learn from them.

What Students Should Expect

The exercises and projects in this book are intended to provide flexibility for students and instructors. Exercises can be used for large and small groups; they can be done individually or in groups; and they may be completed in-class or involve out-of-class work. Requirements vary from exercise to exercise, and project to project—some require presentations and others require written assignments. They also vary in length of time to complete, from only about ten minutes to several hours. The intent has been to prepare a variety of exercises and projects, so the instructor can choose those that are most appropriate for a particular course and group of students; therefore, your instructor will probably not assign all of the exercises or projects, but, rather, those that the instructor feels are most meaningful for students, given the other learning experiences to which they will be exposed.

I encourage students to read and think about all the exercises, even those that may not be assigned. This will add to an overall appreciation of the challenges and complexities of international business management. There are many other issues faced by international companies that could have been included in this book. These exercises should, however, give students an appreciation of the complexity of decisions in companies that are international.

Student Participation and Learning

Learning is always partially a function of participation, but this is particularly true with experiential learning. If a student participates with enthusiasm, learning can be substantial for everyone involved and enjoyable as well. In contrast, if a student chooses not to participate, there will be little benefit for that individual; further, this makes learning more difficult and less enjoyable for classmates. Some students are uncomfortable with this method of learning because they find it unstructured and wonder how much real information can be gained in exercises. If you feel uncomfortable and concerned about this as a means of learning, why not try to "suspend your disbelief," relax, and enjoy the process; then reevaluate it at the conclusion of the course.

EXPERIENCING INTERNATIONAL BUSINESS AND MANAGEMENT

Overview of International Business Management

The following brief description of the major characteristics of international business management will give students a preliminary overview of the context in which the exercises take place. Managing a business in the environment of the early twenty-first century almost certainly involves international aspects. This can range from the small manufacturer that may employ a cross-cultural work force, to the global company that may view anywhere in the world as a source of inputs such as raw materials, labor, capital, expertise, location, and markets. The scope of these two examples is different, but both face an international environment, and neither can overlook its implications.

Successful corporations embrace a global perspective and philosophy to survive and prosper in this international environment. This is a challenge for the organizations of the early twenty-first century. Many will succeed or fail on the basis of their ability to deal with this dynamic environment. International business itself is not new; international companies have existed for a long time. If one goes back to the earliest records of the Egyptians, the Greeks, the Phoenicians, or the inhabitants of the Far East, there are references to business transactions across borders. The difference today stems from rapid advances in transportation and communications technology, which have resulted in relatively fast and easy global movement and communication. This means that virtually all business has some international aspects. Anyone who is involved in the management of a business organization, therefore, needs to be concerned with the international nature of business.

Historical Overview

The post–World War II era has seen a rapid expansion of international business. This internationalization of business is described by Robinson (1981) in terms of the "actors" participating in the process. Following are four major phases that Robinson describes.

Phase 1: World War II to 1955

This phase consists basically of two actors: the firm itself and its foreign commercial constituencies (customers, suppliers, licensees, joint-venture partners, and so on). This was a relatively simple environment, where a company's strategies were largely determined by the company itself, with little concern for groups other than its immediate constituencies. The United States dominated this phase of international business. Whereas Europe and Japan were under reconstruction following the war, the United States was powerful and respected. U.S. technology, machines, and consumer goods were in demand around the world. This led to increased exports at first; but then, when foreign trade barriers were imposed, to foreign direct investment. During this period many less-developed countries or LDCs as they were then called were not yet independent, national policies on foreign investment were still being formed, and those national policies that existed were poorly implemented. This gave international companies virtually free reign in their international activities. It was a time when "American management" was considered superior, even though there were many successful European companies operating internationally. Thus, U.S. companies managed their foreign subsidiaries with U.S. citizens, and training for these international assignments was not considered necessary.

Phase 2: 1955 to 1970

This phase consists of three actors: the firm, its commercial constituencies, and the host government. Many international companies had become large by this phase, with globally integrated production and marketing. U.S. multinational corporations (MNCs) were owned, controlled, and managed by U.S. nationals. Concurrently, many LDCs had become independent and sensitive to the potential loss of sovereignty represented by giant foreign corporations. The more developed nations had formulated policies regarding foreign investment and actors were implementing these consistently. These factors combined to make relations with host governments an important consideration for international companies. Europe and Japan had rebuilt following the war, and European and Japanese companies had increased their presence in the international arena. This meant increased competition for U.S. companies and also provided alternative sources of capital, skills, and technology for host governments. A shift of power from international companies towards host governments occurred, increasing the risks faced by these companies. "American management" was still admired, but there was increasing recognition of the important role of individuals with international expertise in successful international operations.

Phase 3: 1970 to 1980

This phase involves four actors: the company, its constituencies, the host government, and the parent government. During this phase, parent governments increasingly recognized that the activities of their international companies outside of their own boundaries had an impact at home in terms of employment, foreign exchange rates, trade, and so forth. Further, the activities of subsidiaries could have political repercussions important to parent countries. This realization led to increased attempts on the part of parent countries to regulate the foreign activities of their international companies. The international environment had become much more complex than it was in the 1940s and 1950s, and international companies needed to consider their impact on a variety of groups. Understanding and analyzing this environment was recognized as important to successful international operations, and companies began formalizing their approach to assessing the international environment and managing the international operations.

Phase 4: 1980 to Present

This phase can be considered a multiactor phase for international companies. Although Robinson proposed his model originally in the 1980s, the multiactor concept continues to be helpful today. In addition to the previously identified actors, there are now international agencies, religious groups, ethnic groups, and various other interest groups—including terrorists—demanding attention from international companies. At the same time, the expertise of all of the actors in dealing with the international environment is becoming more sophisticated. In addition, international companies in this era can originate from any country of the world.

There is no reason to expect the international environment to become less complex in the future. In fact, the existence of increasingly sophisticated technology worldwide suggests that the international environment will continue to become more complex. This will provide new opportunities and threats for international companies. A complex international environment means that international expertise is vital to the successful operation of many companies. For companies to manage effectively in this complex and changing global environment, they need to be sensitive to the objectives and activities of all the actors now involved. Managers need skills that can help them assess the impact of various international factors on their businesses.

Need for International Expertise

The brief discussion of the phases through which international business has progressed since the 1940s demonstrates its increasing complexity over time. This complexity, stemming from interactions and transactions across national boundaries, is the key difference between international companies and those that are essentially domestic. The choices for the international company are more varied than those available to its domestic counterpart and are, consequently, more difficult to assess. Improved international expertise, useful in all business today, is of growing importance to those companies whose primary opportunities lie in global activities. International management is not different in kind from domestic management; rather, it is different in scope. The same management issues are faced by domestic and international companies, but the solutions may be different.

The Nature of International Business

The complexity of the international business environment means that international ventures are inherently more risky than purely domestic ones. For example, international managers need to consider the political risk of operating in foreign environment, they have to factor changes in foreign exchange values into their decisions, and they have to be aware of how cultural and national forces affect their marketing efforts. These are only a few of the changes that occur as companies move across national borders. All these changes make international business complex and risky. For rational business decisions to justify international activities, therefore, there must be perceived benefits that outweigh the risks. International operations generally can be seen as either proactive or reactive. Proactive international ventures take advantage of perceived opportunities; reactive ventures respond to actions taken by other parties or defend against perceived threats.

The major proactive and reactive motives that account for companies becoming international in their operations are explained in the following discussion (see Exhibits 1 and 2 for a summary). Proactive motives include taking advantage of resource availability, lower costs, and new markets, as well as exploiting firm-specific advantages, incentives, and international tax advantages. Reactive motives include responding to trade barriers, international customers, or competitors, and seeking to avoid home country regulations.

Proactive Explanations

International differences in customs and cultures, and differing factor endowments, provide many opportunities for companies outside of their home borders, as the following list illustrates:

- Resources are available in some locations and not in others; they are easier to access in certain locations, or they can be cheaper and subject to fewer restrictions. This is true of natural, human, and technological resources.
- Costs are lower in some locations than in others. Natural resources are less expensive in locations where they are plentiful, and labor costs are lower where labor is abundant. In addition, transportation and energy costs may differ depending on the location of production and markets. The costs of doing business, including interest rates and taxes, vary from country to country.
- Many governments offer incentives to encourage companies to do business with, or in, a particular country or region. Such incentives offered by host governments include provision of industrial buildings, insurance, tax exemptions, tax holidays, and interest-free loans. Incentives offered by home governments include trade assistance, subsidies, low-interest loans, and risk insurance. These incentives can increase profits and decrease risks, making foreign operations very attractive.
- Different levels of economic development and different life styles, customs, and conditions throughout the world all provide opportunities for new markets in foreign locations.
- A mature product in a declining market at home may be an innovative product in a growth market somewhere else. Outdated technology at home may be welcomed elsewhere. Skills developed in the home market may be transferred to other locations. The opportunities are almost endless.
- Company strengths that originate at home can be equally advantageous in the global environment. A well-known brand name, a technological lead, and a recognized company image are all potential global strengths.
- Tax differentials among countries are important to companies that operate internationally. A company can minimize the corporate taxes that it pays globally by locating its various operations in appropriate countries. A company seeking to maximize its after-tax profits will seek out these opportunities.
- Economies of scale that are not available in a single country may be possible on a larger international basis. In addition, integrated operations may offer a form of synergy through learning from different locations.

Exhibit 1

Proactive Reasons for Engaging in International Business

Additional resources	Various inputs—including natural resources, technologies, skilled personnel, and materials—may be easier to obtain outside of the home country.
Lowered costs	Various costs—including labor, materials, transport, and financing—may be lower outside of the home country.
New/expanded markets	New and different markets may be available outside of the home country, and assets—including management, skills, machinery, and money—may be utilized in foreign countries.
Economies of scale/ synergy	National markets may be too small to support efficient large-scale production, while sales from several national markets combined are more efficient. Synergy can be obtained from transferring learning across national borders.
Exploitation of firm-specific advantages	Technology, brands, recognition, and other firm-specific advantages can all provide opportunities in the global environment.
Incentives	Incentives may be available from the host government or the home government to establish operations or trade relationships with foreign countries.
Tax systems	Different corporate and income tax systems in different countries provide opportunities for companies to maximize their worldwide after-tax profits.

Exhibit 2

Reactive Reasons for Engaging in International Business

Trade barriers	Tariffs, quotas, buy-local policies, and other restrictive trade practices can make exports to foreign markets impractical, and local operations in the foreign location become desirable.
International customers	If the customer base becomes international and the company wants to continue to serve this base, local operations in foreign locations may be necessary.
International competition	If the competition becomes international, and the company wants to remain competitive, foreign operations may be necessary.
Regulations	Regulations and restrictions imposed by the home government can increase the costs of operating at home, and it may be possible to avoid these by establishing foreign operations.

Reactive Explanations

Many companies do not actively seek international involvement; this can be because the risks and costs are seen as too high, the payoffs are seen as relatively low, or the company does not have adequate resources to pursue international opportunities actively. These companies, nevertheless, often find that internationalization is forced on them because of events outside of their control. The following issues illustrate reactive internationalization:

- Trade barriers imposed by trading partners who are customers for a company's product or services often force managers to alter international operations. These trade barriers can make a product or service too expensive for customers in the export market. However, if the product or service is produced in the export market location, it ceases to be subject to the trade barriers. Many companies react to the imposition of trade barriers by setting up operations to serve foreign markets locally.

- If a company's customers choose to become international, the company may have to follow their lead to retain them as customers. Many international companies prefer to deal with one supplier worldwide; thus, if a supplier cannot supply their needs in foreign locations, it may lose them as domestic customers as well.
- If the competition becomes international, a company may have to follow this lead to remain competitive. If international competitors become well-established in foreign environments, this may put them in a position to attack a competitor's domestic market with lower cost products or services. In addition, if competitors become well-established in international markets, the domestic company may find it very difficult to compete in these markets at a later stage. Some companies, therefore, follow the international lead of their competitors.
- Home governments can impose regulations and restrictions that increase the costs of operating. These include environmental, health and safety, and insurance regulations, among others. If less rigorous regulations and restrictions exist elsewhere, other factors being equal, managers may decide to operate in the less restrictive environment.

Forms of Entry into Foreign Locations

A company that has decided to become international can make its entry into foreign markets in a variety of forms ranging from exports and imports, through licenses and contracts, to ownership of foreign operations. The nature of the business activities that a particular company undertakes is a function of that company's specific situation. A simplified way of looking at the decision regarding the form of entry that is appropriate for a particular company is in terms of the following three dimensions:

1. the degree of perceived risk in a particular location;
2. the degree of perceived attractiveness of a particular location; and
3. the company's ability to undertake international operations.

In a positive situation, where risk is perceived as relatively low, the location is perceived as attractive, managers believe they have the ability to undertake the international operation, and the company would want the maximum involvement allowed by law. This would differ from country to country because laws and regulations differ. In a negative situation, where risk is perceived as high, the location is perceived as relatively unattractive, the company is unsure of its ability to expand internationally, and managers would likely decide to avoid this international possibility completely. In mixed situations, decisions reflect strengths and opportunities as well as weaknesses and potential threats. For example, in a risky but attractive environment, a company wants to minimize its exposure while exploiting the market; exports or licensing arrangements might be appropriate. In a safe but relatively unattractive environment, serving the location by exporting surplus domestic production might be all a company would consider. In a safe and attractive situation, where the company considers its abilities weak, a joint venture to augment its resources would be appropriate, as would a program to strengthen its own resources prior to expansion.

Ownership and Partners

Many international ventures involve shared ownership and the choice of partners. Foreign companies may be required by local regulations to have local owners, or they may choose to do so because of the perceived benefits associated with having local input. Companies may also choose to share ownership with other foreign companies.

In general terms, the benefits from sharing ownership are the sharing of risks and the addition of needed resources. Sharing ownership with locals is generally desirable from a local political viewpoint and thus may be less risky. A foreign company may be more accepted because locals are seen as part of the decision-making processes and thus more responsive to local interests. In addition, local ownership ensures retention of some of the benefits of the operation for a host country. Many companies seek local partners because this input provides valuable local information and insight, as well as access to local contacts, which allows the foreign company to be more responsive to local needs.

Sharing ownership with other foreigners may also be desirable from the company's viewpoint because it spreads the risk and supplements resources. The financial burden of international investment can be shared among partners, and host governments may be more unwilling to antagonize many foreigners than one. Other foreign partners are often sought to supply such complementary resources as special skills, capital, and machinery that a company lacks. Foreign partners as described here may be other companies from the home country or companies from a third country.

Shared ownership, in addition to its benefits, has drawbacks. Of most concern to managers is the potential loss of control that accompanies shared ownership. The objectives of the several partners often differ and can lead to conflicts that can be costly. International communication among partners may be difficult, particularly where language differences exist, and getting things done can take a long time.

If shared ownership is necessary or desirable, then the degree of ownership is an important consideration. Ownership in foreign subsidiaries can range from a minority share on the part of the parent company to 100 percent ownership. Partners can range from silent (sharing ownership but not decision making) to fully participating. A company can choose to share ownership with one partner or many. The various options need to be weighed carefully because there are benefits and risks involved in each. To some extent, the choice will be a function of what is legal and practical in a given country; but within these limits there will still be options available.

In essence, the choice among these options must be made in light of protecting a company's particular strategic advantages. This means that protecting and retaining control over certain aspects of a company's business will be of paramount importance to management, and ownership decisions should reflect this. Ownership and control, while interconnected, are not identical. It is important to recognize that host countries can retain control of a subsidiary, through regulation and a host country's sovereign rights, even if the subsidiary is wholly owned by a foreign company. Equally, a company can retain control of a subsidiary in which it has a minority ownership share through its control of technology, markets, supplies, capital, and so forth.

A decision to share ownership also implies the necessity for choosing partners. In some situations, this can involve a relatively simple share offering on local stock markets. In most situations it involves selecting one partner or a small number of partners.

Joint ventures have been likened to marriages; if they are to be successful, partners must be chosen with care. The cost of a joint-venture breakup is high; therefore, managers need to plan carefully to avoid this outcome. Perhaps the most useful advice on choosing a joint-venture partner is to go slowly; consider several partners, consider how well resources complement each other, consider both parties' objectives, and consider the relationship of corporate culture and national culture. Once a partner has been chosen, managers should be specific about the following:

- each partner's contribution to the project;
- each partner's expectations of the project;
- management arrangements;
- goals and objectives;
- performance evaluation measures and processes;
- time frames; and
- conflict resolution mechanisms.

Perhaps most importantly, managers need to understand what happens if things do not go well. Like a marriage, there is often euphoria associated with signing the joint-venture agreement. Managers must look beyond this, and contracts should include specific conditions and provisions for dissolving the partnership, if necessary.

Managing International Operations

The increasingly complex international environment affects all aspects of business. It affects decision making in terms of corporate planning, organizing, and controlling, as well as corporate staffing and management of human resources. All the functions of a business (e.g., marketing, personnel, finance, and operations) are also changed in an international environment. The movement of goods and services, money, and people across national borders makes the management of international operations complex. Operational decisions are made in the context of the national and cultural characteristics of the varying environments in which a company operates.

There is no clear distinction between national and cultural characteristics, but national characteristics are considered to be the more concrete and observable ones that distinguish nation from nation. National characteristics include laws and regulations, economic conditions, and political ideology. They are generally used to describe an entire nation. Cultural characteristics are more abstract and subjective and include values, attitudes, and beliefs. These are often thought of as pertaining to an entire nation, but they may be shared with people of other nations, and there may be different cultures within any nation.

Role of Culture in International Management

The abstract nature of culture makes it difficult to identify and analyze; any examination of culture is therefore simplistic and must be understood in this context. The model in Exhibit 3 is useful in understanding the relationship between cultural antecedents, values, and manifestations. This model suggests that both national and societal variables contribute to societal culture, which is expressed in terms of individual values; these values in turn influence

Exhibit 3   **Simplified Model: Cultural/National Variables and Organizational Behavior**

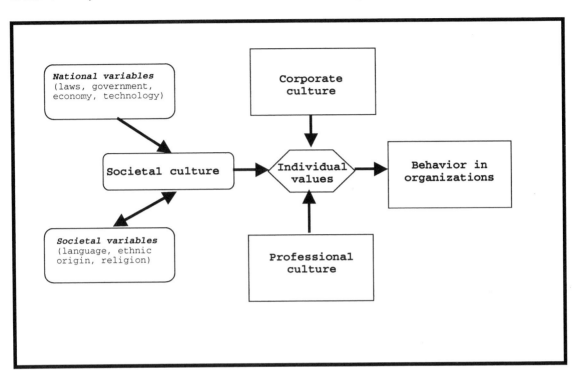

individual behavior. Individual behavior is important to the organization in all of its operations; thus, managers who operate internationally must try to understand the various cultures within which it operates.

Societal culture is a function of both national and societal variables. Individual values are a function of societal culture, as well as corporate and professional cultures. Individual behavior in organizations depends, at least partially, on the values held by individuals. A useful method for analyzing cultures is in terms of their relative similarity or dissimilarity. Exhibit 4, using information from Ronen and Shenkar (1985), presents clusters of countries based on the similarities of their cultural values; cultural values, in this context, are the shared preferences of a national grouping.

In general, operating in culturally similar countries can be expected to be relatively easy, whereas operating in culturally dissimilar countries can be expected to be relatively difficult. Operations in similar countries can incorporate many of the home country procedures, while operations in dissimilar countries will have to adapt procedures or develop new ones. Decisions regarding the standardization or adaptation of management procedures need to be made in light of particular cultural values. One of the most useful models that has been developed for assessing cultural values proposes four cultural value dimensions (Hofstede 1980). These dimensions are described as follows.

Individualism/Collectivism

Individualism/Collectivism (IDV) is the degree of emphasis given to the individual compared with the degree of collectivity that prevails in a society. In a society high on individualism, there is an emphasis on individual achievement, leadership, and decision making.

Exhibit 4

Country Clusters Ranked on Similarities of Values

Cluster	Countries
1. Anglo	Canada, Australia, New Zealand, United Kingdom, United States
2. Germanic	Austria, Germany, Switzerland
3. Latin European	Belgium, France, Italy, Portugal, Spain
4. Nordic	Denmark, Finland, Norway, Sweden
5. Latin American	Argentina, Chile, Colombia, Mexico, Peru, Venezuela
6. Near Eastern	Greece, Iran, Turkey
7. Far Eastern	Hong Kong, Indonesia, Malaysia, Philippines, Singapore, South Vietnam, Taiwan
8. Arabic	Bahrain, Kuwait, Saudi Arabia, United Arab Emirates
9. Independent*	Brazil, Japan, India, Israel

Source: Adapted from Ronen and Shenkar (1985).

Notes: The countries listed in this table are those that have been included in research studies. Many countries of the world are thus not included. Countries within a cluster are considered similar with regard to their cultural values. Clusters are arranged in an approximate order of cluster similarity; that is, the Anglo cluster is more similar to the European clusters (Germanic, Latin European, and Nordic) than it is to the Latin American, Near Eastern, Far Eastern, and Arabic clusters. A major limitation of these clusters is that they are based on empirical studies which, at that time, did not include Africa, much of Asia, and Eastern Europe. Asia has received more attention recently (see Hofstede 1991), but Africa and Eastern Europe still have not been studied extensively.

*Not closely related to other countries.

Individuals have a right to their own opinions, want autonomy on the job, and owe their basic allegiance to themselves and their immediate family. The United States is an example of a society high on individualism. In contrast, in a society low on individualism, or high on collectivism (e.g., countries in Latin America and the Far East), the emphasis is on group achievement and decision making. Social needs are high and the group provides support for the individual.

Uncertainty Avoidance

Uncertainty Avoidance (UAI) is the degree to which ambiguity and uncertainty are accepted and tolerated by society. In a society high on uncertainty avoidance, there is a lack of tolerance for uncertainty or ambiguity; people prefer and need formal rules and structure and do not readily accept deviance. In contrast, in a society low on uncertainty avoidance, uncertainty and dissent are accepted; there are fewer rules, they are less conservative, change is accepted readily, and generally they are more accepting of differences.

Power Distance

Power Distance (PDI) is the degree of acceptance and formalization of inequality in society. In a society high on power distance, the order of inequality is well-defined, and one's place in society is known and accepted. Society and organizations are hierarchically structured with a clear delineation of power. In contrast, in a society low on power distance, equality is seen as desirable and all people have equal rights. While power differences exist, they are seen as changeable.

Masculinity/Femininity

Masculinity/Femininity (MAS) is the degree to which traditional male values are accepted by society. In very masculine societies, the male values of assertiveness, money, and possessions predominate. Gender roles are clearly defined and manliness is admired. In feminine societies (societies low on MAS), female values of nurturance, sympathy, and service predominate. Gender roles are fluid and both manliness and femininity are admired. Exhibit 5, using information presented by Punnett and Ronen (1984), presents similarities and differences in cultural antecedents among these clusters of countries. Cultural antecedents, in this context, refer to the national and cultural variables that are believed to shape cultural values.

This value framework has been used in a number of research studies, and data exist for a wide variety of cultures and nations for comparative purposes. Exhibit 5 summarizes the data presented by Hofstede for countries grouped according to the clusters previously identified. Countries are described as being high (H), moderately high (MH), moderately low (ML), or low (L) on each of the value dimensions. These descriptions were derived by dividing the Hofstede scores into quartiles.

This information on cultural values is useful in understanding different cultures in which a company operates. It is, however, only one model of culture and is not intended to be comprehensive. In addition, this societal framework is not meant to imply that all people of a culture will be alike. Managers can use this cultural information as a starting point, but they will need to complement this information with more detailed, culture-specific information.

One approach that incorporates culture-specific information into the management process takes situations considered to be universally encountered by managers (e.g., discipline, evaluating performance, leadership, motivation) and asks host-country managers to identify, from their cultural perspective, the most effective means of dealing with such situations. This approach, while time-consuming and costly, can pay off for international companies (Punnett 1989).

International Organizational Structures

International firms need international structures to facilitate their achievement of international strategies. The appropriate structure will depend on the company's strategy. From a broad, general perspective, international structures can take many forms; examples include export divisions, international divisions, international functions, international product management, international regions, and international matrix. One can think of companies evolving through several structural changes as they shift from a domestic to a global focus. A typical path of development might be as follows.

Stage One: This stage occurs when the company's exports become too large for a domestic unit to handle efficiently; this leads to the establishment of an export division.

Stage Two: This stage occurs as international sales increase, and the company establishes foreign branches or subsidiaries; this leads to the establishment of an international division.

Stage Three: This stage occurs as international sales and operations become as large as domestic sales and operations; this leads to the establishment of a global or worldwide structure, such as:

Exhibit 5

Cultural Value Indices for Countries, Grouped by Cluster

Cluster	IDV	UAI	PDI	MAS
Anglo				
Australia	H	ML	ML	MH
Canada	H	ML	ML	MH
Ireland	MH	L	L	MH
New Zealand	H	ML	L	MH
South Africa	MH	ML	ML	MH
United Kingdom	H	L	ML	MH
United States	H	ML	ML	MH
Germanic				
Austria	MH	MH	L	H
Germany	MH	MH	ML	MH
Switzerland	MH	ML	ML	H
Latin European				
Belgium	MH	H	MH	MH
France	MH	MH	MH	ML
Italy	H	MH	ML	H
Portugal	ML	H	MH	ML
Spain	MH	MH	MH	ML
Nordic				
Denmark	MH	L	L	L
Finland	MH	ML	ML	L
Norway	MH	ML	L	L
Sweden	MH	L	L	L
Latin America				
Argentina	ML	MH	ML	MH
Chile	L	MH	MH	L
Colombia	L	MH	MH	MH
Peru	L	MH	MH	ML
Venezuela	MH	MH	L	H
Near Eastern				
Greece	ML	H	MH	MH
Iran	ML	ML	MH	ML
Pakistan	L	MH	MH	MH
Turkey	ML	MH	MH	ML
Far Eastern				
Hong Kong	L	L	MH	MH
Philippines	ML	ML	H	MH
Singapore	L	L	H	ML
Taiwan	L	MH	MH	ML
Thailand	L	MH	MH	ML
Independent				
Brazil	ML	MH	MH	ML
India	ML	ML	H	MH
Israel	MH	MH	L	ML
Japan	ML	H	MH	H

Source: Adapted from Punnett and Ronen (1984).

Notes: IDV = Individualism/Collectivism; UAI = Uncertainty Avoidance; PDI = Power Distance; MAS = Masculinity/Femininity. H = high (1st quartile); MH = moderately high (2nd quartile); ML = moderately low (3rd quartile); L = low (4th quartile).

- a global *functional* structure where such functions as marketing and finance are standard worldwide (this is often used by resource-based companies such as oil companies);

- a global *product management* structure, where product lines require specialized R&D, production, marketing, and support functions, and primary international management responsibility is for similar product clusters;
- a global *area* structure where only a few product lines are produced and sold in many countries and where products must be customized for each area, and primary international management responsibility is for an area;
- a global *matrix* where many product lines are produced and sold in many countries, and products need to be customized to local conditions and markets, and primary international management responsibility encompasses both product clusters and areas.

Consider the following firms and their likely choice of structure:

1. a pharmaceutical company with manufacturing operations in twenty-three countries and sales in forty-eight countries. The company manufactures and sells a major line of painkillers, as well as a small number of specialty drugs. This firm probably would select a form of international regional structure.
2. an oil company conducting R&D, exploration, extraction, refining, wholesaling, and retailing operations worldwide—this firm probably would select a form of international functional structure.
3. an accounting firm with 20 percent of business outside of the United States through associates in five countries. Clients are mainly North American MNCs, with overseas operations. This firm probably would have an international divisional structure.
4. a manufacturing company with sales and manufacturing facilities in fifteen countries. The company manufactures a wide range of products, from electronic parts to sports equipment. This firm probably would select a form of international matrix structure.
5. a retail company with stores specializing in fashion, sports equipment, hardware, and office furniture, located in the United States; it also exports to Canada. This firm probably would simply opt for an export division.

Summary

The complexity of international management decisions means it is often difficult to understand them, from a practical point of view, within a classroom setting. The purpose of this book is to give students an opportunity to address international decisions in a simulated real-life setting. The exercises included here encompass the major management processes in international management, as well as the various business functions. These exercises are limited in number, and, therefore, many subtleties of international management are not covered. Rather, the intent of these exercises is to give students an appreciation of decision making in an international environment. The exercises provided are intended to cover a range of issues and to provide choices on some issues. Instructors may choose to use only a few of the exercises. Students may be interested in working on others, on their own or in groups. Many provide a helpful means to consider a new topic or to review a past topic. Most importantly, students and instructors should approach this text as one that is intended to bring alive the subject of international management.

References

Hofstede, G. *Cultures Consequences: International Differences in Work Related Values.* Beverly Hills, CA: Sage, 1980.

Kolb, David A. *Experiential Learning: Experience as the Source of Learning and Development.* Englewood Cliffs, NJ: Prentice-Hall, 1984.

Punnett, B.J. International Perspectives on Organizational Behavior and Human Resource Management. Armonk, NY: M.E. Sharpe, 2004.

Punnett, B.J., and S. Ronen. "Operationalizing Cross-Cultural Variables." Paper presented at the 44th Annual Meeting of the Academy of Management, Boston, August 1984.

Robinson, R.D. "Background, Concepts and Philosophy of International Business from World War II to the Present." *Journal of International Business Studies* 12, no. 1 (Spring/Summer 1981): 13–22.

Ronen, S., and O. Shenkar. "A Clustering of Countries on Attitudinal Dimensions: A Review and Synthesis." *Academy of Management Review* 10, no. 3 (1985): 435–54.

Exercises

Exercise 1

Defining an International Company

Aim

This exercise can be a good introduction to the topic of international business. It also can be used to help you summarize what has been learned about international companies.

Time

This exercise should take students about 30 minutes of outside preparation and about 60 minutes of class time.

Assignment

Individual: Imagine that you can categorize companies as "domestic" or "international." Do some library/Internet research on the differences between domestic and international companies and make a list of the characteristics of an organization that would probably differ for domestic and international companies; be as exhaustive and imaginative as possible.

Group: Discuss the characteristics identified by group members. The group should decide which characteristics are most useful and develop a list of criteria to be used for judging whether or not a company is international. Please use the worksheet provided. For example, your group might consider "ratio of foreign sales to domestic sales" an important distinguishing characteristic and decide that once a company reaches foreign sales of 20 percent of total sales, it should be considered international. Once your group has decided on a list of characteristics and criteria, move on to the rest of the exercise. Here you are asked to develop a definition of an international company and to consider if there are degrees of internationalism; that is, do you feel it is helpful to distinguish between a multinational, an international, a transnational, and a global company? Use the Worksheet for Exercise 1 on the next page to address these issues.

Worksheet for Exercise 1

Name(s): _____   Date: _____

_____

Part 1. Distinguishing Between a Domestic and an International Company

	Measurement criteria	Characteristics
1.		
2.		
3.		
4.		
5.		
6.		
7.		
8.		
9.		
10.		
11.		
12.		
13.		
14.		
15.		

Part 2. Definition

Use the space below to formulate a definition of an international company. (This definition should be a synthesis of the characteristics and measurement criteria identified in Part 1.)

Exercise 2
Moving from Domestic to Global

Aim

The objective of this exercise is to consider different forms of internationalization and ways in which a company might normally develop over time.

Time

This exercise will take about 90 minutes of class time, or it can be assigned as an individual, out-of-class exercise. If the exercise is to be done in class, students should bring to class their definitions of the forms of entry as identified below.

Group Assignment

Picture a small, family-owned and managed firm that manufactures specialized dolls and sells these dolls locally. The firm is initially a purely domestic firm. Use the Worksheet for Exercise 2 provided to identify a pattern of international entry for this firm. Include the following forms of international entry in your discussion: wholly-owned subsidiaries, global integration, proactive exports, licensing, reactive exports, joint ventures, and strategic alliances. Define each form of entry and describe its advantages and disadvantages. Hand in a group worksheet.

Individual Assignment

Using the same worksheet, complete the exercise above individually. Hand in an individual worksheet.

Worksheet for Exercise 2

Name(s): _____   Date: _____

_____

Definitions of International Forms of Entry

Wholly-owned subsidiaries: _____

Global integration: _____

Proactive exports: _____

Licensing: _____

Reactive exports: _____

Joint ventures: _____

Strategic alliances: _____

Advantages and Disadvantages of International Forms of Entry

	Advantages	Disadvantages
Wholly-owned subsidiaries:		
Global integration:		
Proactive exports:		
Licensing:		
Reactive exports:		
Joint ventures:		
Strategic alliances:		

Exhibit 6   **Internationalization Over Time**

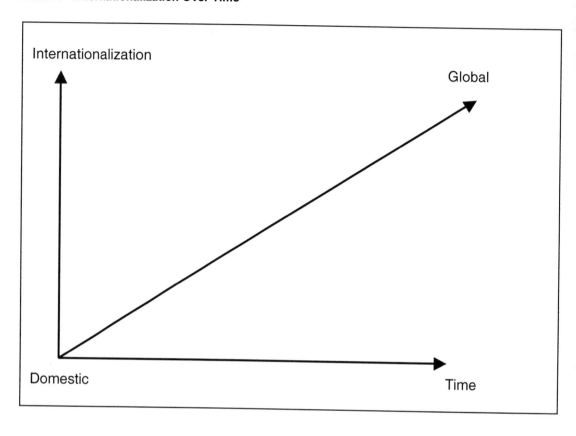

International Development Over Time

Use Exhibit 6 to plot the likely international development (internationalization), from domestic to global over time.

Exercise 3
Benefits of Trade

Aim

This exercise demonstrates the potential benefits that can accrue from trade.

Time

The exercise takes about 30 minutes of class time.

Assignment

The class will be divided into five groups of three or four students. Each group will begin with ten units of one good. Goods can be either products or services. The goods are labeled A, B, C, D, and E. Each group will attempt to increase its wealth by trading goods with other groups on a one-for-one basis; that is, if the group gives up one unit of A, it gets one unit of B, or for two units of A it gets two units of B, and so on. The group's aim is to maximize its wealth. Use Exhibit 7 to calculate the value of goods as described below.

Note that the value of each unit of a good is a function of how much of that good you already own; that is, the more of any good that you have, the less each additional unit is worth. For example, as shown in Exhibit 7, one unit of A is worth $5,000; two units are worth $9,000 or $4,500 each.

If your group gives up one unit you lose some value; this must be balanced against what you gain by trading. For example, if you have ten units of A and give up one, you lose $100 (you go from ten units to nine, or from $17,100 to $17,000); if you trade for B and if you have no units of B, you gain $2,000 (you go from zero units to one, or from $0 to $2,000). Your group gains $1,900 in this trade. Alternatively, if you have six units of A and give up one, you lose $800 (you go from six units to five, or from $15,800 to $15,000); if you trade for B and if you have six units of B, you gain $600 (you go from six units to seven, or from $8,400 to $9,000). Your group loses $200 on this trade.

The instructor will provide each group with ten units of a good to begin with; each group should record the beginning value of the ten units that it has been assigned. Each good is

Exhibit 7

Value of Goods Based on Number of Units

Units	A$	B$	Goods C$	D$	E$
1	5,000	2,000	6,000	4,000	3,000
2	9,000	3,900	11,000	7,500	5,500
3	12,000	5,400	15,000	10,000	7,500
4	14,000	6,600	18,000	11,500	9,000
5	15,000	7,600	19,000	12,500	10,000
6	15,800	8,400	19,900	13,200	10,800
7	16,400	9,000	20,700	13,700	11,500
8	16,800	9,400	21,400	14,000	12,100
9	17,000	9,600	22,000	14,200	12,600
10	17,100	9,700	22,500	14,300	13,000

represented by a different letter, A–E. The group will have five minutes to discuss its strategy as a group; the group may decide to trade as individuals or as a group, but gains or losses will accrue to the group. Groups will then trade, following its chosen strategy, with the other groups. Goods must be traded on a one-for-one basis only: If a group gives up one unit of a good, it gets one unit of another in return. Each group's objective is to maximize the group's wealth. The instructor will announce when to start trading and when to stop. Each group will recalculate its wealth at the end of the trading period and determine its gains or losses.

Exercise 4
Trade Considerations

Aim

The purpose of this exercise is to examine various trade agreements between and among countries, given certain cultural characteristics. The exercise demonstrates that trade is a function of many factors, not only a country's comparative advantage.

Time

The exercise takes about 45 minutes of class time.

Assignment

The class will be divided into five groups of three to six individuals. Each group will represent a specific country—Alpha, Beta, Gamma, Delta, or Epsilon. Each country has a specific number of a particular product to sell at a specified cost. The following data describe the products, costs, objectives, and constraints for each country.

Country Alpha

Product:	Aircraft
Cost:	$5 million each
Quantity available:	Five
Goal:	Maximize profit
Constraints:	1. Need cattle—at least eight herds
	2. Must sell all aircraft—no domestic use

Country Beta

Product:	Trucks
Cost:	$1.5 million each
Quantity available:	Fifteen
Goal:	Import advanced technology
Constraints:	1. Need three aircraft urgently
	2. Want five computers and two herds of cattle

Country Gamma

Product:	Cattle
Cost:	$1 million per herd
Quantity available:	Twenty herds
Goal:	Access to a wide variety of products
Constraints:	1. Cattle are sacred
	2. Alcohol is forbidden

Country Delta

Product:	Computers
Cost:	$2 million each
Quantity available:	Eight
Goal:	Maximize exports
Constraints:	1. Cannot trade with Country Beta
	2. Want three aircraft

Country Epsilon

Product:	Wine
Cost:	$0.5 million per shipment
Quantity available:	Thirty shipments
Goal:	Maintain good relations with trading partners
Constraints:	1. Cannot produce beef locally
	2. Must arrange transportation for purchases

Each group's assignment is to trade with other groups to try and reach its objective, given its particular products, costs, and constraints. A group may trade with one group and receive a product that it does not need in order to use it in trading with another group. Groups may barter goods or pay for them with currency. The instructor will provide groups with currency and goods. At the conclusion of the exercise, each group will evaluate its position in terms of its original goals and constraints.

Worksheet for Exercises 3 and 4

Name(s): _____   Date: _____

_____

Please respond briefly to the following questions.

1. Were you surprised by the results of Exercise 3? Why were you surprised or not surprised?

_____
_____

2. What do you feel is the main lesson of Exercise 3?

_____
_____
_____
_____
_____
_____
_____
_____
_____

3. How does Exercise 4 differ from Exercise 3?

_____
_____
_____
_____
_____
_____
_____
_____

4. What do you feel is the main lesson of Exercise 4?

_____

_____

_____

_____

_____

_____

_____

_____

Exercise 5
Choosing Your Suppliers

Aim

This exercise will give students the opportunity to assess a variety of options that might be available to a small company seeking international sources of supply. It also gives students an opportunity to work out an agreement with a foreign supplier.

Time

This exercise will take about 30 minutes of class time.

Background

The case involves a small North American company that wants to purchase supplies from a developing country. The company supplies fishnets and other fishing supplies to the Great Lakes commercial fishing industry. Mr. Perch, the president, started the company after several years as a commercial fisherman. Perch recently visited a trade show where he had the opportunity to observe some nets manufactured in South Korea. The price of these nets compared favorably with those made in North America—$4.00/sq. ft. versus $12.00/sq. ft. The South Koreans have not exported nets to the United States or Canada; thus, Perch sees an opportunity to gain a price advantage over the competition. He orders a small quantity of the nets on a trial basis; this involves considerable effort in terms of arranging letters of credit, transportation, clearing customs, and so on—but it seems well worth the effort if a cheap source of supply is the result.

The South Korean company is excited about the prospect of a possible export market. Market research suggests that there is a large potential market for the products in the United States and Canada and that they enjoy a considerable cost advantage over competitors from North America.

The trial shipment arrives in North America and Perch finds that the nets are unsuitable for use in freshwater lakes—they were designed for use in the ocean. Upset and angry, he contacts the South Korean company to express his misgivings. In the meantime, he becomes aware of a variety of other potential sources of the supply, including the Philippines, Indonesia, and various Caribbean islands. The South Korean company is confused by this turn of events. The company is interested in pursuing this export opportunity but does not have the expertise necessary to manufacture nets that are appropriate for freshwater fishing. The Korean government is also interested in the export opportunity and has indicated a willingness to provide export incentives for the company.

Assignment

The class is divided into an even number of small groups. Half of the class represents the North American company; half represents the South Korean company. Each group discusses the situation among themselves and decides on an appropriate course of action; each group then meets with a counterpart group (e.g., the North American company meets with the South Korean) to decide on a detailed agreement. A spokesperson representing each pair of groups is chosen to report the details of the agreement to the class. Each group wants to maximize the benefits from its perspective; at the same time the groups are seeking a win/win solution that will be satisfactory to all parties. Each group should consider the following issues: continuity of supply, quality assurance and warranty, transaction currency and method of payment, exclusivity, credit and financing.

Worksheet for Exercise 5

Name(s): _____   Date: _____

_____

Please briefly complete the following sections.

1. Outline the agreement reached.

_____

_____

_____

_____

_____

_____

_____

_____

_____

_____

_____

2. Which side (South Korean or North American) do you feel got the best deal? What accounts for this?

_____

_____

_____

_____

_____

_____

_____

_____

_____

_____

_____

3. What was the most difficult point to negotiate? Why was this particularly difficult?

_____

_____

_____

_____

_____

_____

_____

_____

_____

Exercise 6

Friendly Negotiations

Aim

This exercise is intended to give you some experience at conducting international negotiations, when conditions are friendly.

Time

The exercise will take about 50 minutes of class time.

Background

Mongo, a large developing nation with friendly relations with the United States, has recently found that it has extensive reserves of PRT. PRT is a newly discovered mineral that cures certain types of cancer. PRT is available in a number of other locations worldwide, but it is difficult to mine in these areas. Mongo's PRT appears to be relatively easy and cheap to obtain. Mongo is eager to make the best possible use of this mineral but does not have the local expertise necessary to mine, refine, and sell PRT effectively; thus, it has been looking for a partner. A U.S. company, Global Pharmaceuticals, has extensive mining and pharmaceutical interests, including some experience mining and selling PRT. The U.S. company believes it has developed a fairly high level of expertise in PRT mining and would like to increase its involvement in PRT mining and selling. Both sides are anxious to reach an agreement regarding exploitation of Mongo's PRT for their mutual benefit. Estimates suggest that yearly sales could exceed US$500 million once full production is reached and that net profit margins could be as high as 10 percent of sales.

Assignment

Divide the class into an even number of small groups of three to five individuals. Half the groups represent the country of Mongo; half represent the Global Pharmaceuticals Company. Meet as a small group for 20 minutes to discuss the situation described and decide on your bargaining position. Then meet with a counterpart group for 20 minutes to negotiate an agreement. Each set of two groups will then describe their agreement to the rest of the class.

Worksheet for Exercise 6

Name(s): _____   Date: _____

_____

Please respond to the following questions.

1. Outline the agreement reached.

_____
_____
_____
_____
_____
_____
_____
_____
_____
_____

2. Which side (the company or the country) do you feel got the best deal? What accounts for
   this?

_____
_____
_____
_____
_____
_____
_____
_____
_____

3. Explain, using this example, why developing countries seek foreign direct investment, and why these countries may also have reservations about such investment.

_____

_____

_____

_____

_____

_____

_____

_____

Exercise 7
How Do You Negotiate?

Aim

This exercise is intended to give you some experience at conducting international negotiations when conditions are not so friendly.

Time

The exercise will take about 60 minutes of class time.

Background

Naire is a developing nation in Africa that has recently elected a socialist government. Allcool is the Nairean subsidiary of a large multinational company headquartered in the United States. Allcool produces alcohol and tobacco products for local consumption. The company had operated profitably in Naire for ten years.

Following recent elections, the new government of Naire has nationalized all foreign-owned companies, including Allcool. A new state corporation has been created to run Allcool, and members of the political elite have been put in charge of operations. This is based on their support of the new government rather than experience in the alcohol or tobacco industries, and the company soon encounters difficulties.

Specific problems include:

- employment levels rising from 1,200 to 1,600 employees;
- production falling from 4,000 to 1,000 cartons of cigarettes and from 3,000 to 900 cases of liquor;
- decreasing quality—rejects up 15 percent, and customer complaints up substantially;
- lack of foreign exchange to purchase needed foreign supplies and machinery; and
- profits falling from 12 to –9 percent of sales.

41

Naire also encounters other difficulties, specifically:

- trade balance deficits;
- lack of foreign exchange;
- external debt arrears;
- government instability;
- high unemployment;
- high inflation; and
- no real growth in GNP.

At the time of nationalization, the Allcool company was valued by its parent at US$4 million. The government of Naire offered to pay US$1 million in compensation. The Allcool parent refused this offer but assumed an attitude of cooperation toward the government. The company felt it stood a better chance of reaching a reasonable settlement by pursuing a cooperative strategy, and it wanted to be ready to resume control if the opportunity presented itself.

The government of Naire has expressed a desire to win back the confidence of foreign investors and has instituted new investment incentives in addition to making overtures to previous investors. The Allcool company believes there may be an opportunity to reestablish itself in Naire and has agreed to a meeting with the government.

Assignment

The class is divided into an even number of small groups of three or five individuals. Half the groups represent the country of Naire; half represent the Allcool company. Meet as a small group for 20 minutes to discuss the situation described and decide on your bargaining position. Then meet with a counterpart group for 30 minutes to negotiate an agreement. Each set of two groups will then briefly present their agreement to the rest of the class.

Worksheet for Exercise 7

Name(s): _____   Date: _____

_____

Please respond to the following questions.

1. Why would a country like Naire decide to nationalize foreign-owned companies?

_____

_____

_____

_____

_____

_____

_____

_____

2. Why would a country decide to invite foreign companies to invest?

_____

_____

_____

_____

_____

_____

_____

3. If a country wants foreign investment but is concerned about the potential negative impact of such companies, what options does it have?

_____

_____

_____

_____

_____

_____

_____

4. If a company is investing in a country where political risk is high, what options does it have?

_____

_____

_____

_____

_____

_____

_____

Exercise 8

The Relative Value of Money

Aim

This exercise is intended to give you practice at calculating the effect of exchange rates on currency values and to help you identify forces that influence exchange rates. Please use the worksheet provided in the Worksheet for Exercise 8 to hand in your investment decisions.

Time

This exercise will take only a few minutes of class time.

Assignment

This is an individual exercise that you will complete largely outside of class. You may work with others on the exercise if you wish.

Imagine that you have US$1 million, which you can invest in the currency market for a four-week period. Spend one week deciding how to invest this money. You may buy as few or as many currencies as you want, or you may keep it as U.S. dollars. Using the Worksheet for Exercise 8, identify your specific investment in writing, giving exchange rates at that time, and hand in the completed worksheet to your instructor.

For example, A, B, C represent different currencies that you have selected.

A	$500,000	@ $0.80 = US$400,000
B	$200,000	@ $1.50 = US$300,000
C	$1,000,000	@ $0.30 = US$300,000

At the end of four weeks (or a time frame specified by the instructor), you will change your foreign currency holdings back into U.S. dollars and calculate the value as well as how much you have made or lost. Use the worksheet provided for your calculations. Some students may wish to buy and sell currencies throughout the period. If you choose to do this, keep track of all your transactions. Some students may also want to buy and sell financial derivatives. If you choose to do this, keep track of your transactions.

Worksheet for Exercise 8

Name(s): _____   Date: _____

_____

Currency bought	Quantity	Exchange rate	Total in US$

Maximum total _____US$1 million

Currency sold	Quantity	Exchange rate	Total in US$

Total for all sales _____

Initial investment _____

Gain or loss _____

Briefly explain your rationale for selecting the currencies you bought and the reasons why these currencies either gained or lost value.

Rationale:

_____

_____

_____

_____

_____

Reasons for gains in value:

_____
_____
_____
_____
_____
_____

Reasons for losses in value:

_____
_____
_____
_____
_____
_____

Exercise 9

Exchange Rates, Investment Decisions, and Balance of Payments

Aim

This exercise is intended to illustrate the relationships among exchange rates, investments, and overall economic transactions between countries.

Time

This exercise will involve outside preparation and about 30 minutes class time. This can be completed as an individual exercise or in a group of three or four students.

Assignment

Before class, identify the various accounts included in a country's balance of payments statements and the transactions that affect balances in each account. Find the current value of the Canadian dollar relative to the U.S. dollar. Imagine a small consulting firm located in southwestern Ontario in Canada, very close to the Canada–U.S. border. The company has a number of clients in the United States and has been considering establishing a small subsidiary there. The president believes that an office in the United States would be profitable, but the company has a policy of allocating no more than 25 percent of its expansion budget to one country. This policy is based on the belief that expansion should not be tied to only one location. The company has an expansion budget of approximately Can$500,000. The firm has assessed the needed investment in a U.S. subsidiary to be approximately US$150,000.

Worksheet for Exercise 9

Name(s): _____   Date: _____

_____

Please discuss the situation described and respond to the following questions (show any calculations that you do to reach your decisions).

1. If Can$1 is worth US$0.80, will the Canadian company invest in the United States? If the value changes to US$0.85, will the company invest?

_____

_____

_____

_____

_____

_____

_____

2. At what exchange rate will the company's decision change from "invest" to "don't invest"?

_____

_____

_____

_____

_____

_____

_____

3. At today's exchange rate, what decision would the company make?

_____

_____

_____

_____

_____

_____

4. How do the company's decisions relate to the balance of payments accounts?

_____

_____

_____

_____

_____

_____

_____

Exercise 10
Advertising Campaigns

Aim

This exercise is intended to help students consider some of the cultural and national issues that affect advertising campaigns.

Time

This exercise will involve outside preparation and about 60 minutes of class time.

Assignment

You will work in small groups of four to six. Your group will be assigned a particular country to consider in terms of an advertising campaign. Your group will develop an advertisement to be used in your country, and you will present this to the class, explaining your rationale for selecting certain media, images, and sounds.

Your group represents a manufacturer of a line of sunglasses ranging from inexpensive to expensive. You are trying to expand your export sales and have identified the assigned country as a potential market. You must decide how to advertise the product; specifically, you should identify a target market, product price range, and positioning and media strategy, considering such factors as climate, disposable income, regulations, media availability, cultural values, and so on. Once you have identified the factors you consider important, you will develop a specific advertisement to be used in promoting your product.

Your advertisement should be designed for a particular media—one that you have identified to be a major part of your advertising campaign. You should include slogans, drawings, voices, and so forth, as appropriate, describing models, voiceovers, and music if they cannot be included in your presentation.

Each group will present their advertisement to the class with a brief explanation. The rest of the class will then be asked to evaluate it on a scale of 1 to 5 using the evaluation sheet provided. Your instructor will summarize these evaluations and provide feedback to each group during the next class. Each group will hand in a written assignment that consists of "copy" for their advertisement, backed up by an explanation of why this particular format was chosen. This should be brief—your aim is to persuade the instructor that your advertising copy will be effective in your country given your chosen target market, local customs, regulations, etc.

Worksheet for Exercise 10

Name(s): _____   Date: _____

_____

Evaluation of Advertisements

Try to put yourself in the position of the target market being addressed and evaluate the effectiveness of the advertisement presented on a scale of 1 to 5 where 1 = excellent, 2 = very good, 3 = good, 4 = fair, and 5 = poor. Please make brief comments to indicate what you like most and least about the particular advertisement being evaluated.

Group   Country   Evaluation   Comments

1. _____

_____

_____

_____

_____

2. _____

_____

_____

_____

_____

3. _____

_____

_____

_____

_____

4. _____

_____

_____

_____

_____

5.

6.

Exercise 11

Expatriate Assignment and Repatriation

Aim

The purpose of this exercise is to demonstrate many of the complex issues that arise when choosing parent country nationals (PCNs) to send to other countries. This situation is examined both from the perspective of the company selecting candidates for a foreign assignment and that of the individual considering such an assignment.

Time

The exercise takes approximately 60 minutes, or about 80 minutes when a written assignment is included.

Preparation

The instructor will assign selected countries to review prior to conducting the exercise. These countries will be used in the exercise.

Format

The class will be divided into an even number of small groups, with three or four students per group. Half of the groups represent a company choosing a manager for an expatriate assignment; their task is to design a package of transfer conditions that they will offer to the prospective expatriate. The other groups represent the prospective expatriate; their task is to decide what they would require to accept the overseas assignment.

Assignment

This exercise is designed to make you aware of the issues faced by companies when selecting and training candidates for overseas assignments, as well as the concerns of candidates accepting such assignments. There are many aspects of such assignments that should be considered if the foreign assignment is to be successful.

The company must consider such things as selection, training, compensation, evaluation, communication, and repatriation. The company will want to ensure that the assignment is successful and will want to minimize the cost associated with the transfer.

The candidate will want to consider the implications of the move from both career and personal points of view. He or she will want to maximize the net benefits associated with the transfer.

You are asked to make decisions regarding a transfer. These decisions, corporate and individual, are often made by people with little international experience—people just like you. There are no right or wrong choices, so feel free to suggest anything your group deems appropriate.

The instructor may provide you with specific countries to examine prior to class, or you may be asked to select a country of interest to investigate. Please use the worksheet provided to summarize your recommendations as company or your requirements as candidate.

Worksheet for Exercise 11

Name(s): _____   Date: _____

_____

Please respond briefly to the following.

1. As a candidate selected to go to _____, what are your main requirements?

_____

_____

_____

_____

_____

_____

_____

_____

_____

_____

2. As a human resource manager, sending someone on assignment to _____, what are your main recommendations?

_____

_____

_____

_____

_____

_____

_____

_____

_____

Exercise 12

Social Responsibility: It Depends on Your Point of View

Aim

This exercise is designed to illustrate the complexity of "socially responsible" decision making. Students will recognize that two groups may take opposing views on the same issue and that each group will justify its view as socially responsible.

Time

This exercise takes about 45 minutes of class time.

Background

The XYZ company, a North American company, has extensive and profitable operations in LMN, a country that North Americans view as violating the basic human rights of a large section of its population. The company is faced with the decision of whether or not it should continue its operations in LMN. The decision is similar to that faced by American companies that had operations in South Africa during apartheid.

Assignment

The class will be divided into three groups. One group represents the board of directors of XYZ; they must make a decision regarding operations in LMN. A second group represents management in LMN, a mix of North Americans and local LMN managers; they believe that XYZ should maintain operations in LMN. The third group represents an activist group in North America; they believe that XYZ should pull out of LMN. Some individuals may be assigned as observers. Each group has a specific assignment:

Group 1: Board of directors—You are to develop criteria that you will use to make your decision. You will listen to the arguments presented by the other two groups and make a decision on the basis of the criteria you develop.

Group 2: Management of XYZ in LMN—You are to develop arguments to present to the XYZ board of directors to persuade the board to continue its operations in LMN. You will also have the opportunity to respond to the activist group; therefore, you should consider your response to the arguments it is likely to present.

Group 3: Activist group—You are to develop arguments to present to the XYZ board of directors to persuade the board to pull out of LMN. You will also have the opportunity to respond to the local management group; therefore, you should consider your response to arguments they are likely to present.

Observer—You are to observe one group; note the decision-making process and the dynamics of the group during its discussions. Complete the worksheet provided for Exercise 12, and be prepared to report to the class on your observations.

Procedure

The discussion will proceed as follows:

1. Each group will have 15 minutes to discuss its position internally and develop its arguments.
2. The management group and the activist group will then be called on to present their positions to the XYZ board; they will have 5 minutes each. The board may ask for expansion of points if it wishes, in which case it may be permitted an additional 5 minutes.
3. There will be a 5-minute period for each group to reconvene and review what has been presented.
4. The board will then call on each of the two groups for responses to the other's arguments.
5. The board will meet briefly to make a decision.
6. The board will explain its decision criteria to the two groups and present its final decision.
7. Observers will report on their observations.

Worksheet for Exercise 12

Name(s): _____   Date: _____

_____

Each student should spend a short time thinking about their role in the exercise, then respond to the questions below. Observers will be asked to describe the process they observed.

Role: _____

1. How do you personally feel about the role you were asked to play—were you comfortable with this role?

_____

_____

_____

_____

_____

_____

2. Do you agree or disagree with the position you were asked to take? Why do you agree or disagree with this position?

_____

_____

_____

_____

_____

3. Do you think international managers should consider social issues when making business decisions? Explain your position.

_____

_____

_____

_____

_____

_____

Observer's Report

Please use the space below to make notes on the process.

Decision-making process: How did members of your group make decisions (e.g., did some-one take a leadership role, did they seek consensus, did they vote, how long did they take, and so on)?

_____

_____

_____

_____

_____

_____

_____

_____

_____

_____

_____

_____

Interactions and dynamics: How did the different groups interact with each other (e.g., did they argue their case effectively, what kind of tactics did they use, was there conflict, and so on)?

_____

_____

_____

_____

_____

_____

_____

_____

_____

_____

_____

_____

Exercise 13
Environmental Concerns and Advocacy

Aim

The purpose of this exercise is to demonstrate an international strategic decision that involves more developed and poorer countries and that is influenced by ethical considerations. Students are asked to consider their personal moral convictions in the context of a particular company decision and also from different stakeholders' perspectives. In addition, students are asked to put themselves in an advocacy position and to persuade another group to accept the position put forward by their group.

Time

The exercise takes approximately 60 minutes.

Background

Students might want to review material on government objectives in developing countries prior to class. The instructor will decide whether or not this preparation is necessary for your class. Imagine the following situation: Both the United States and Canada have simultaneously banned production and use of the pesticide ABC; the ban is the result of demonstrated harmful effects to certain species of plants and animals in the wilderness and an apparent potential for causing cancer in humans. ABC is very effective in controlling certain pests that do extensive damage to crops. The production and sale of ABC has been profitable for the XYZ company, and the company has stocks of ABC that can no longer be sold in North America. The XYZ company has been approached by a lesser developed country, LMN, with two propositions. First, LMN is willing to buy the existing stocks of ABC at a reduced price; second, LMN is willing to offer incentives for the XYZ company to manufacture ABC locally in LMN.

There are many options available to XYZ. The appropriate choice among options is a function of the cost–benefit tradeoff as perceived by various constituencies and according to the individual's subjective assessment of the situation. You are asked to express your own reaction to the situation as a member of a particular group concerned with the company's decision.

Assignment

The class will be divided into five stakeholder groups. Group 1 represents shareholders; group 2 represents the interests of the company employees; group 3 represents the potential customer—LMN; group 4 represents a concerned citizen group in North America; group 5 represents a concerned citizen group in LMN.

Consider the company's options—be exhaustive—and how each option could affect your group. You should decide as a group which option you wish the company to choose; then formulate a series of arguments that could be used to persuade the company to adopt your point of view. Finally, consider how your choice will be affected if XYZ is struggling for profitability and ABC is its main product.

This exercise will give you a feeling for how different stakeholder groups may view the same situation and how individual, personal views can affect strategic decisions. You will have a period of about 30 minutes to discuss and formulate the position of your group. Each stakeholder group will then be asked to present its position, chosen course of action, and arguments for following that course of action. When each group has presented its decision and arguments, a second round of discussion will be conducted. There will be a brief discussion, within each group, of the various positions that have been presented; then each group will have the opportunity to respond to the suggestions of the other groups and raise counterarguments.

Worksheet for Exercise 13

Name(s): _____   Date: _____

_____

Role: _____

1. Please identify the options for the company and their impact on your group.

_____
_____
_____
_____
_____
_____
_____
_____
_____
_____
_____
_____
_____

2. Disregarding your assigned role, what do you as an individual feel would be the best decision for the company?

_____
_____
_____
_____
_____
_____
_____
_____
_____
_____
_____
_____

Exercise 14
Child Labor and International Managers

Aim

This exercise will give students an opportunity to consider how they would feel if their company operated in a country where child labor was common. This exercise puts students in a position where their personal beliefs may be in conflict with corporate practices.

Time

The exercise will take about 45 minutes of class time.

Background

Consider the following: In many parts of the world where poverty is extreme, child labor is legal and accepted. Children in these places often work in factories, under relatively unpleasant conditions, and they may work long hours. These children may not receive any education, and limited healthcare is available to them. Nevertheless, the work that these children do enables their families to survive. Their meager wages contribute to the family's food and shelter. Their parents may be unable to work themselves or may need to stay home to care for other family members, grow some crops, raise animals, and so on. In other words, there is little choice for the working children and their families; their survival depends on their labor. Moreover, by having some children work, others can be educated; and the educated child or children eventually will earn more money than would be possible otherwise, which will contribute to the family moving out of poverty.

Many human rights advocates in wealthier countries have called for a worldwide ban on child labor. The former president of the United States, Bill Clinton, used his State of the Union Address to call for the abolition of child labor. Most people living in more developed countries are uneasy with the idea of child labor, and there have been consumer boycotts of companies that employ children.

Now imagine this scenario: You are a manager in a multinational firm visiting a subsidiary in the Far East to establish new safety measures in the subsidiary. When you first arrive at the factory, you are shocked to see that many of the employees are, in fact, children. Some appear to be as young as 10 years old. You ask the local manager of the factory why this is allowed. She explains that employing children is the normal practice in that area and that the children work willingly. You ask what happens about the children's education, and she says that there is little need for education for the jobs they do, and that, in any case, education is limited in this region. Similar answers are given about healthcare—if children are injured at work, they are sent to the local clinic, which is about a mile away.

You return to your hotel with modern and luxurious accommodations and try to relax in the swimming pool, but you cannot put the picture of the young children working in the factory out of your mind. You must decide how to proceed with your assignment, and you need to consider what recommendations to make to headquarters in the United States.

Assignment

As individuals, respond to the questions in the Worksheet for Exercise 14. Meet with a counterpart, or in small groups, to discuss each person's reactions to the situation. Decide on the best approach to this situation.

Worksheet for Exercise 14

Name(s): _____   Date: _____

_____

Individually consider and respond to the following issues.

1. If you were a child working to help your family survive, how do you think you would feel?

_____

_____

_____

_____

_____

_____

2. If you were the parents of a working child, how do you think you would feel?

_____

_____

_____

_____

_____

_____

3. If you were manager of this subsidiary, how do you think you would feel?

_____

_____

_____

_____

_____

_____

4. What options does the international manager have?

_____

_____

_____

_____

_____

_____

5. What would you personally recommend in this situation?

_____

_____

_____

_____

_____

_____

Exercise 15
Describing Culture

Aim

This exercise is intended to familiarize students with the concept of "culture." This exercise may be assigned as homework or it can be completed in class.

Time

It should take about 80 minutes to complete.

Assignment

This exercise may be assigned as an individual exercise, a small group exercise, or discussed by the class as a whole. This exercise can be completed without outside reading, but readings on culture can be helpful, and your instructor may assign specific readings in preparation. The following issues will be addressed: defining culture, identifying aspects of culture, and comparing nations with cultures.

Worksheet for Exercise 15

Name(s): _____   Date: _____

_____

Please respond to the following, either individually or in small groups.

1. Define the word "culture" in a few sentences.

_____
_____
_____
_____
_____
_____
_____
_____
_____
_____

2. Identify aspects of culture that might be of interest to an international company, and give examples to illustrate the importance of these various aspects.

_____
_____
_____
_____
_____
_____
_____
_____
_____
_____

3. Explain (a) how a nation is similar to a culture and (b) how a nation is different from a culture.

_____

_____

_____

_____

_____

_____

_____

_____

_____

_____

Exercise 16
Diversity and Cross-National Management

Aim

The purpose of this exercise is to explore what we mean by diversity and how diversity is likely to relate to managing in different countries.

Time

This exercise will take about 30 minutes to complete, followed by 15 minutes of discussion.

Assignment

In groups of three, please consider the following questions, and respond using the worksheet.

1. What do we mean by "diversity" in the workplace? (Give a definition of diversity.)

2. What aspects of diversity are you likely to find in the workplace in your home country? (Give examples.)

3. How do you think people generally react to diversity in the workplace?

4. What do you see as the benefits of working with a diverse group?

5. What do you see as the problems of working with a diverse group?

6. How do you think diversity will affect you as an international manager?

Worksheet for Exercise 16

Name(s): _____   Date: _____

_____

1. What do we mean by "diversity" in the workplace? (Give a definition of diversity.)

_____
_____
_____
_____
_____
_____
_____
_____

2. What aspects of diversity are you likely to find in the workplace in your home country?
   (Give examples.)

_____
_____
_____
_____
_____
_____
_____
_____

3. How do you think people generally react to diversity in the workplace?

_____
_____
_____
_____
_____
_____
_____

4. What do you see as the benefits of working with a diverse group?

_____

_____

_____

_____

_____

_____

_____

5. What do you see as the problems of working with a diverse group?

_____

_____

_____

_____

_____

_____

_____

6. How do you think diversity will affect you as an international manager?

_____

_____

_____

_____

_____

_____

Cross-Cultural Leadership Style

Aim

This exercise is intended to help you understand how culture affects leadership styles and practices.

Time

The exercise will take about 60 minutes, 10 minutes individually and 50 minutes in a group.

Assignment

This exercise involves specific cultural value concepts and leadership styles. Students will need to review information on culture and leadership prior to doing the exercise. Any good . text on international or cross-cultural management should include the cultural information, and any basic text on management or organizational behavior will include the information on leadership. In *International Perspectives on Organizational Behavior and Human Resource Management* (M.E. Sharpe, 2004), Betty Jane Punnett discusses both culture and leadership.

Individually make some notes in response to the questions below. In groups of three or four, share your views and discuss the questions. Complete the Worksheet for Exercise 17 as a group.

Discussion Questions

1. In a society that is high on power distance and femininity, what kind of leadership style would you expect to find?
2. What kind of society would probably encourage leaders to be autocratic? What kind of society would encourage them to be participative?
3. How would "teamwork" function in a highly individualistic society?
4. In a society where relationships are lineal, and people are believed to be either good or bad, what kind of leadership style would you expect to find?

Worksheet for Exercise 17

Name(s): _____   Date: _____

_____

1. Describe a society that is high on power distance and femininity.

_____

_____

_____

_____

_____

Explain the leadership style that would be effective in this culture.

_____

_____

_____

_____

_____

2. Explain how autocratic and participative leaders behave.

_____

_____

_____

_____

_____

Autocratic:

_____

_____

_____

_____

_____

Participative:

_____

_____

_____

_____

_____

Describe a society that would encourage leaders to be autocratic.

_____

_____

_____

_____

_____

Describe a society that would encourage leaders to be participative; try to think of more than one cultural dimension that might influence this leadership style.

_____

_____

_____

_____

_____

3. Describe what is meant by "teamwork."

_____

_____

_____

_____

If a society is highly individualistic society, explain how teamwork would function.

_____

_____

_____

_____

4. Describe what a lineal society would look like.

_____

_____

_____

_____

_____

Describe a society where people are believed to be either good or bad (not changeable).

_____

_____

_____

_____

_____

Explain the leadership style you would expect to find in a society that is both lineal and that believes people are not changeable.

_____

_____

_____

_____

_____

Exercise 18
Cross-Cultural Motivation

Aim

This exercise is intended to help you understand how culture affects motivation.

Time

This exercise should take about 90 minutes of class time. Your instructor may assign some of the work to be done at home.

Background

Consider the following situation: There is a developing country, Gamma, where people are relatively poor. Some facts about Gamma follow:

- In Gamma, people like to work closely in groups. They do not believe people should make decisions on their own; rather, they seek consensus of all group members. Gammans are often seen in groups discussing what they should do next.
- In Gamma, strict hierarchies are observed. People are born to a certain level or station in life and are expected to remain there. In organizations, managers are expected to make decisions and instruct their subordinates. Lower-level Gammans accept orders without question.
- In Gamma, people believe that they have little control over their environment. The expression "God willing" describes the general attitude towards personal responsibility and action. Gammans behave in ways they think are acceptable to society and higher authority.

Assignment

In small groups, discuss how a particular motivational theory would apply in the country Gamma. The process will be as follows:

1. Select a motivational theory (e.g., Maslow, Equity, Expectancy, Reinforcement) to examine.
2. Briefly describe the major elements of the selected theory as presented in an organizational behavior text.
3. Examine each element of the theory in light of the description of Gamma, and try to identify how the culture of Gamma as described would influence the theory.
4. Does your group think the theory could be used to motivate people in Gamma? If it can be used, would you propose any modifications to the theory? If it cannot be used, what are the theory's main limitations?
5. Write a skit to illustrate your selected theory in Gamma. In your skit one person will represent a North American, and one person a Gamman. The North American will try to explain the theory to the Gamman, and the Gamman will respond from a Gamman perspective.
6. Each group will present its skit to the class.

Worksheet for Exercise 18

Name(s): _____   Date: _____

_____

Motivational theory selected: _____

Brief description of the main tenets of this theory:

_____
_____
_____
_____
_____
_____
_____
_____
_____
_____
_____
_____

Brief explanation of why this theory would or would not work in Gamma:

_____
_____
_____
_____
_____
_____
_____
_____
_____
_____

Exercise 19
Cross-Cultural Awareness Quiz

This quiz is not intended to teach you specific lessons about different cultures but, rather, to make you aware of the many subtle, and not so subtle, issues that need to be considered when moving cross-culturally.

1. You are in Tokyo with two colleagues from headquarters in Canada, negotiating a sale of Barbados rum. There are eight Japanese negotiators. How many foreigners are there?

    _____ eight   _____ two   _____ one   _____ three

2. You are in Rio de Janeiro making inquiries about local suppliers. You speak some Spanish but not very well. What would you do?

    _____   Make an attempt to speak Spanish with your contacts.
    _____   Concentrate on speaking English very slowly and distinctly.

3. You are introduced to the following people:

    Ling Sing Chee, in Singapore: _____

    Hayashi Masaki, in Japan: _____

    Robert Alright, in England: _____

    Atipol Chungsamarnyart, in Thailand: _____

    Thomas Bennett, in the United States: _____

    Tommy Ho Chin, in Taiwan: _____

How would it be appropriate to address them? Write your response after each name.

Special thanks to Prof. Lorna Wright of York University (Canada), formerly affiliated with Queens University, for providing many of the quiz items used here.

4. What greeting would you use in which country?
   a. a firm handshake   ____ Japan
   b. a wai   ____ Germany
   c. a gentle handshake   ____ Indonesia
   d. a bow   ____ Thailand

5. You have just arrived in Kuwait; which of the following gifts would be inappropriate to offer your host? Why?
   ____   a small ornament depicting a dog;
   ____   a bottle of Barbados rum;
   ____   a book of "Miss World" beauties in bikinis; or
   ____   a book of "thoughts for the day" drawn from the Bible.

6. You have just arrived in China; which of the following gifts would be most appropriate to offer your host? Why?
   ____   a calendar of dogs and cats;
   ____   a traveling alarm clock;
   ____   a set of stamps commemorating Canadian–Chinese relations; or
   ____   all gifts are inappropriate.

7. You are in Japan, and your host presents you with a colorfully wrapped box, which is clearly intended as a personal gift. What would you do?
   ____   Thank him profusely and open the box.
   ____   Thank him profusely and put the box away carefully.
   ____   Thank him, and present him with a gift in return.
   ____   Tell him that you are sorry, but you are not allowed to accept gifts.

8. When would you present a business gift in the following countries—on the first meeting, on the second meeting, at the end of negotiations, never, on a special occasion?

   China   _____
   Japan   _____
   Ireland   _____
   Saudi Arabia _____
   Belgium   _____

9. You have been meeting with a local Arab agent in the Middle East and have spent several hours socializing and drinking coffee. No business has been discussed, and you are anxious to get discussions underway. What would you do?
   ____   Raise the subject when there is a lull in the conversation.
   ____   Wait for him to raise the matter.

10. It is time for you to leave the Arab agent, and you have still not discussed any business. You feel frustrated. What would you do?

_____ Tell him your meeting has been a waste of time.

_____ Ask if you can leave a set of materials for him to review.

_____ Ask him when you can return to see him.

11. You are in Thailand reviewing a project that is way behind schedule. You can find no good reason for the delays. You are asked to give your reaction to the Thai manager and staff of the project. What would you do?

_____ Tell them the rate of progress is awful, and that if they do not "pull up their socks," they will be "sacked."

_____ Ask them collectively the reasons for the delays.

_____ Go through the aims and history of the project, point out the difficulties, and praise them for overcoming these difficulties, so the project can now go on as planned.

_____ Ask the project manager to explain why the project is behind schedule and ask him what he will do about it.

12. You are negotiating a sale of rye to China. They want to buy 10,000 cases over the next two years and may double that order if your price is lower than their current supplier. Your usual price is $500 per case. What would you do?

_____ Offer a trial discount of $400 per case hoping to get the larger order.

_____ Tell them your price is $500 per case, and there is no possibility of lowering the price.

_____ Quote a price of $550 per case so there is room for negotiation.

13. What does "table the point" mean?

in England: _____

in Canada: _____

in the United States: _____

14. You are in Riyadh and visit the local bazaar. You go to a money-changers booth and find there is no one there; however, there are large stacks of different currencies clearly visible and easily accessible. In a few minutes, the money changer returns to serve you. What would you think?

_____ that the man is inviting a robbery;

_____ that there must have been a sudden emergency; or

_____ that this must be normal business practice here.

15. Which of the following would you *not* do in which country?

    a. Present a gift with your left hand.   _____ Australia

    b. Give the thumbs up signal.   _____ Japan

    c. Make a circle with your thumb and forefinger.   _____ Kuwait

    d. Give a letter opener as a gift.   _____ Latin America

16. Which foods are not likely to be served in which countries?

    a. steak   _____ Israel

    b. pork   _____ China

    c. cheese   _____ India

17. How are dogs treated in the following countries?

    Korea   _____

    Kuwait   _____

    Jamaica   _____

    Canada   _____

    the United States   _____

Exercise 20

Cultural Scenarios

Aim

The purpose of this exercise is to illustrate that the way we react "at home" to various situations may be considered incorrect in other locations. The simple scenarios described provide an opportunity to discuss the differences one may encounter in foreign locations.

Time

This exercise will take about 30 minutes of class time.

Assignment

Individually, consider the following scenarios, and then respond based on how you would react at home.

1. You meet a Japanese colleague for the first time and exchange business cards. What do you do with your colleague's business card?

   a. Put it in your pocket for future reference.
   b. Study it carefully, then put it on the table in front of you.
   c. Use the back to make notes about special issues that arise.

2. You are at a Chinese banquet, and your host keeps serving you food from the central platter. How do you react?

   a. Eat what you are given to be polite.
   b. Eat some of what you are given, but not all, because you know there are more courses to come.
   c. Politely refuse because you are concerned about the germs in the central dish.

3. You are meeting an Arab colleague, whom you have met before but do not know well. After you have greeted him, what should you do?

    a. Accept the coffee that you are offered.
    b. Ask politely about his wife and family.
    c. Get down to business as quickly as possible.

4. You are in Mexico for a brief business meeting with a company representative. The meeting takes place at a local Tappas Bar. When the representative arrives, what would you expect?

    a. to have a couple of drinks and talk about Mexico;
    b. to order drinks and then get down to business so you can get it done quickly;
    c. to have one quick drink and then adjourn to an office to discuss business.

5. You are visiting the Far East and a business associate and her family are showing you around. Her daughter, a small child, makes a cute comment. What would you do?

    a. Pat her on the head, and say, "How cute!"
    b. Kiss her on both cheeks to express your appreciation of her comment.
    c. Ignore her because children should not speak in the company of adults.
    d. Respond reservedly, "Your child is very intelligent."

6. You have asked an Indian colleague for his opinion on a proposal. He says, "I really like the idea" and nods somewhat up/down and left/right. You conclude that:

    a. He is being polite but does not really agree.
    b. You offer alternatives because he obviously does not agree.
    c. You go on to the next point, confident of his agreement.

Exercise 21
Stereotypes and Foreign Practices

Aim

The first part of this exercise is based on a joke circulating in Europe. It illustrates the fact that stereotypes can be either positive or negative. It also illustrates how easy it is to stereotype groups of people. We do it all the time and need to be aware of the stereotypes we hold and how they affect our thinking. The second part of this exercise gives you a chance to try out new behaviors.

Time

This exercise will take about 20 minutes of class time.

Assignment

Part 1.

This exercise takes the form of a game. As individuals, you are asked to match nationalities and tasks in the context of the European Union (EU). The countries are Britain, France, Germany, Italy, and Switzerland. The roles are government workers, engineers, cooks, lovers, and policemen.

Several countries of the EU are trying to decide what role each should play in the community. There is some disagreement among the countries, so they decide to play a game. First, they will assign tasks as they would be assigned in Heaven; then, they will assign tasks as they would be assigned in Hell. You are asked to put yourself in this position and create the assignments using the Worksheet for Exercise 21. Your instructor will provide you with the view of "Heaven" and "Hell" as seen by the Europeans.

Your view of heaven will reflect what tasks you think the people of each country perform well, and your view of hell reflects what tasks you think they do not perform well. As you review these stereotypes, consider how they would affect your interactions with someone from the particular country.

Part 2.

The second part of this exercise asks you to actually try out some new behaviors, as follows:

   In parts of Latin America, people conversing stand closer together than they do in North America. In pairs, students should talk to each other and establish a "normal" distance; they should then move closer together, and see how they feel at a closer distance, and how long they can comfortably maintain the closer distance. In Latin America, students can practice the reverse (i.e., standing further apart).

   In parts of the East, it is considered impolite to meet the eyes of the person to whom you are speaking. Students should carry on a conversation without making eye contact, and see how they feel about this. Representing countries where not making eye contact is normal, students can practice the unfamiliar (i.e., making eye contact).

   In parts of the Middle East, it is common to sit cross-legged on the floor for extended periods. Students can try sitting in this position, and see how long it is comfortable (this may be done outside of class and reported on later). Alternative positions can be used, such as squatting; sitting in a straight backed, upright position; lounging; and so on.

Worksheet for Exercise 21

Name(s): _____   Date: _____

_____

Stereotypes

In my view of heaven, roles would be assigned as follows:

<u>Country</u>	<u>Role</u>
Britain	_____
France	_____
Germany	_____
Italy	_____
Switzerland	_____

In my view of hell, roles would be assigned as follows:

<u>Country</u>	<u>Role</u>
Britain	_____
France	_____
Germany	_____
Italy	_____
Switzerland	_____

Exercise 22
Managing Political Risk

Aim

This exercise is intended to familiarize you with various aspects of international operations that are generally classified as managing political risk.

Time

This exercise may be assigned as homework, or it can be completed in class. It should take about 80 minutes to complete.

Assignment

You will complete this exercise on your own; this will be followed by a class discussion where individuals will be called upon to contribute their ideas on the various topics. Please use the Worksheet for Exercise 22 to:

1. Formulate a definition of political risk.
2. Identify specific aspects of political risk.
3. Identify characteristics of a country that make it risky.
4. Identify characteristics of a company that might make it politically risky.
5. Suggest ways for the company to manage risk.

This exercise can be completed on your own without outside reading, but readings on political risk are helpful. Your instructor may assign specific readings in preparation for the exercise.

Worksheet for Exercise 22

Name(s): _____   Date: _____

_____

1. I would define political risk as:

_____
_____
_____
_____
_____
_____

2. In assessing political risk, I would consider the following factors:

_____
_____
_____
_____
_____
_____

3. I think of a country as risky if the following factors are true of that country:

_____
_____
_____
_____
_____
_____

Give examples of countries you would consider politically risky.

_____
_____
_____
_____
_____
_____

4. I think a company is subject to political risk if the following factors are true of the company:

_____

_____

_____

_____

_____

_____

5. If your company were involved in a situation that you felt to be personally risky, what would you do to minimize your exposure to risk?

_____

_____

_____

_____

_____

_____

Exercise 23
Risk Assessment and Management

Aim

The purpose of this exercise is to consider assessing and managing risk where risk is seen as substantial. Students select a country where they believe there is a substantial degree of political risk, and determine how they would manage a firm's exposure to risk in this country.

Time

There is outside preparation for this exercise and it takes about 90 minutes of class time. Alternatively, the entire exercise can be done outside of class.

Individual Assignment

Outside of class, each student identifies a country that is considered politically risky and does a preliminary assessment of this country, based on published risk indices, recent events, and news reports.

Group Assignment

In class, students form groups of four. Group members share information on the countries they have investigated, and select one to review in more detail. Groups assume that they represent the political-risk department of a medium-sized firm called "International Management Incorporated" (IMI). IMI has decided to establish a subsidiary in the country being established, in spite of the high level of risk (the benefits have been assessed as outweighing the risks). IMI is a consulting firm specializing in market assessment, using a variety of proprietary computer simulation programs. Complete the Worksheet for Exercise 23 and hand it in to your instructor.

Worksheet for Exercise 23

Name(s): _____   Date: _____

_____

1. Identify the risks that IMI faces in the country (terrorism, government takeover, local hostility, onerous regulations, currency collapse, and so on).

_____
_____
_____
_____
_____
_____
_____

2. Decide how to structure the subsidiary to minimize IMI's exposure to risk. Consider, but do not limit your discussion, to the following: ownership structure, management makeup, legal protection of proprietary assets, debt/equity structure, relationships with parent and other subsidiaries, insurance, human resource policies, marketing, public relations.

_____
_____
_____
_____
_____
_____
_____

3. Give a brief summary of your risk-management strategy.

_____
_____
_____
_____
_____
_____
_____

Exercise 24
What is Bribery?

Aim

This exercise gives students an opportunity to consider the advantages and disadvantages of making a payment that appears to be a bribe and to consider when "extra" payments are considered bribes and when they are not.

Time

The exercise will take 20 to 45 minutes.

Background

Consider the following situation: Investment-U.S. is a company headquartered in the United States. The company has recently entered into a trade agreement with an Indian company. The Indian company has agreed to act as representative for the U.S. company on the basis of product information provided by Investment-U.S., as well as government incentives provided by the Indian government. Mr. Smith, marketing vice-president of Investment-U.S., is in India to ensure the success of the project. He is surprised to find that the initial shipment has been held up in customs because government import restrictions have not been complied with, due to insufficient data. The information, which is vital to the implementation of the agreement, had been supplied previously by the U.S. head office. Smith is approached by a junior clerk in the Indian company, who explains that his predecessor was very disorganized and that the material has probably been misfiled. The clerk suggests that if he were to work overtime, he could probably find the material, but the Indian company does not pay for overtime, and the clerk wants to be appropriately recompensed.

Assignment

Complete the Worksheet for Exercise 24 and hand it in to your instructor.

Worksheet for Exercise 24

Name(s): _____   Date: _____

_____

Put yourself in Mr. Smith's position. You feel you are being asked for a bribe.

1. Would you agree to the payment? Why or why not?

_____
_____
_____
_____
_____
_____

2. What are some of the consequences of making the payment?

_____
_____
_____
_____
_____
_____

3. What are some of the consequences of not making the payment?

_____
_____
_____
_____
_____
_____

4. Would your answer be different if the payment were $5 versus $500?

_____
_____
_____
_____
_____
_____

5. Do you think a tip in a restaurant could be considered a bribe?

_____

_____

_____

_____

_____

_____

6. Anticorruption legislation often distinguishes between a "grease payment" and a bribe. Discuss what you see as the difference between these payments.

_____

_____

_____

_____

_____

_____

Projects

The following projects depend largely on work outside of class, although presentations and discussion may take place in class as well.

Project 1
Country Profiles

Project 1 gives students valuable practice at finding information on countries and putting this information into a useful format. This project also gives students the opportunity to investigate countries that may be of particular interest to them. It involves work almost exclusively outside of class, but students will be required to present their country profiles to classmates, either as a class presentation or as a written assignment.

Students will choose one or more countries to investigate. Students can use the list below as a guide but should not be constrained by these subject areas; any information that is potentially relevant to international management decisions should be included in the profiles.

History;
Geography;
Climate;
Demography;
Economy;
Government;
Foreign relations;
Industrial production;
Business practices;
Infrastructure;
Life style;
Social systems.

Following are some suggested sources of information for this project:

Academic American Encyclopedia;
Business International Comparative Statistics;
Economist Intelligence Units;
Encyclopedia Americana;
Hofstede, G., *Cultures Consequences* (Beverly Hills, CA: Sage, 1980);
Micropedia Ready Reference;

Moody's International Manual;
PriceWaterhouse Information Guide;
The New Encyclopedia Britannica;
United Nations Economic Surveys;
World Book Encyclopedia;
World Tables;
Yearbook of International Trade Statistics;
Yearbook of National Accounts Statistics.

The suggested sources can be used, but, again, do not feel limited to these sources only. Students should be sure to document all sources used in obtaining information.

There are also many Internet sites that provide country information, and most countries now have their own Web sites. Internet sites are a valuable source of information, but they need to be used with some caution. For example, most country Web sites are prepared with a particular aim in mind—to attract visitors, to attract investors, to promote exports, and so on—and necessarily the sites may exhibit a certain bias. Students are encouraged to make use of a variety of sources and to consider primary sources as well as secondary sources. Interviews with people from the country being researched can provide insights that may not be available through published media.

Students may be asked to present their country information as a poster, and the class will host a "poster session" to allow participants to learn about business opportunities in different countries.

Project 2
Export Decisions

Project 2 gives students the opportunity to look at potential export markets and make decisions regarding addressing such markets. Students will work in groups. Each group will be assigned a product to investigate and a country to consider as an export market. Each group will compile information on its product, and potential market, and make a decision regarding the viability of exporting to that market. In addition, each group will decide which export route would be most appropriate for its product/market; for example:

> *Home country agents*: export houses, resident foreign buyers, export association, export brokers

> *Foreign country agents*: individuals, import brokers, distributors, sales branches

Groups should consider the following factors in making their decisions:

- Potential market size and attractiveness;
- Export and import tariffs, quotas, restrictions;
- Transportation and distribution channels;
- Advertising and media;
- Exchange rates and currency fluctuations;
- Political risk.

In addition your discussion should answer the following questions:

1. Who will be the customer(s)?
2. How attractive is this potential export market and why?
3. What payment arrangements would you accept?

Students may be asked to do an oral presentation of their findings, as well as a written presentation.

Project 3
Investment Decisions

Project 3 gives student the opportunity to apply theories and models regarding investment decisions to a realistic situation. Students will work in groups, and each group will consider a real international company. Information may be in the form of a published case study, or the group may be required to do research on the company. Each group will also be assigned two countries to consider for investment. The group will decide which market it wants to enter and how it proposes to enter (e.g., joint venture, wholly-owned subsidiary, conglomerate, license, franchise, and contract). Presentations will take the form of a task force presenting findings to top management.

The following questions to consider can be used as a guide in making investment decisions.

Questions to Consider

1. *Should the company expand internationally?*

- effect on home market
- competitors' activities
- customers' needs
- potential markets
- potential suppliers
- cost differentials

2. *Is the company capable of expanding internationally?*

- management
- money
- products
- marketing
- equipment

3. How attractive is the location?

- size
- per capita income
- income distribution
- accessibility
- degree of competition
- friendliness
- resource costs
- available skills
- incentives

4. How risky is the situation?

- economic stability
- government stability
- terrorism
- restrictions
- government/business relationships

5. How much involvement is desirable?

This is a trade-off between attractiveness and risk. As attractiveness increases and risk decreases, involvement becomes more desirable, and vise versa. If a location is very attractive, and the perceived risk is low, then maximum involvement is sought. If the location is not very attractive, and the perceived risk is high, then minimum or no involvement is appropriate. In intermediate cases the specific risks and attractions are considered before deciding what moderate involvement is most appropriate.

6. What specific form of entry is appropriate?

Consideration should be given to the legal situation, regulations, incentives, and the degree of control required in order to decide on the specific form of entry (e.g., license, franchise, contract, joint venture, strategic alliance, greenfield investment, acquisition, and merger).

Project 4

Individual Personal Profiles

The individuals depicted in these profiles are fictitious. They represent people who might work for the same company—a fictitious company identified as BJP—at a variety of positions and at various levels. The profiles are summary descriptions that might have been prepared from information the company has on file, plus individual's statements of interest in foreign postings and comments from fellow employees. They are intentionally brief but not unrealistically so; in making international assignment decisions, one often begins with fairly limited information.

The information in the profiles includes age, marital status, family, education, religious affiliation, and experience with the company prior to joining it. Some comments regarding personality and reasons for considering the individual for an overseas assignment are also included. Because the information is limited, in some cases you may wish to make inferences or assumptions about a particular individual.

The profiles do not include detailed information on the individual's job-related or technical skills. You should make the assumption that the individuals are technically competent for a particular assignment and base your assessment on other factors that might affect individuals in various foreign assignments.

Students will work in groups for this project. Consider that your company, headquartered in the United States, is selecting employees to send to the following countries: Japan, Saudi Arabia, Brazil, the United Kingdom, South Africa, and India (the instructor may choose to assign different, or additional, countries). Read the ten personal profiles on the following pages, and decide who you will select for each country. These profiles can be used for a variety of additional exercises and projects that your instructor may assign.

Assess each candidate in terms of general suitability for an overseas assignment as well as for assignment to a particular country. Be specific about the factors in favor of an assignment as well as those against an assignment. When a candidate is not selected for an assignment, be specific as to why the candidate was eliminated.

Profile 1
Sandy Merrifield

Gender:	Female
Age:	25
Marital status:	Single
Religious affiliation:	Practicing Roman Catholic
Family:	Sandy lives alone in an apartment in New York City; parents run motel in Florida
Education:	B.A. in English literature
Languages:	Has studied and "understands," but does not speak, Spanish
Experience:	Joined BJP's Packaging Division on graduation from college three years ago; worked as secretary to the marketing manager for two years; promoted to assistant to the marketing manager eleven months ago
International experience:	Belonged to an international students' organization while at college; spent six months as a volunteer social worker in Ethiopia
Personality:	Outgoing, well-liked by fellow workers
Hobbies:	Skiing, hiking, bicycling; is a member of a local synchronized swimming team
Additional information:	Has not traveled internationally other than to Ethiopia; expresses a particular interest in an overseas position because it will give her an opportunity to see the world

Profile 2
Clarke Jenkins

Gender:	Male
Age:	36
Marital status:	Married
Religious affiliation:	Active member of Baptist Church; expresses deep religious values
Family:	Black Guyanese parents live in England; wife is Canadian of British descent, actively involved in volunteer work with several community charitable organizations; two children, ages seven and nine
Education:	British high-school education with A-level qualifications; Bachelor of Commerce from major Canadian university; MBA from small college in New York State
Languages:	Speaks French and Swahili
Experience:	Joined BJP's head office two years ago as assistant to the vice president of Finance; prior to that, he worked with an accounting firm in Canada for five years
International experience:	Worked with a consulting firm in Jamaica (West Indies) for four years
Personality:	Described by supervisor as open to new ideas; describes himself as sensitive to cultural differences
Hobbies:	No information available
Additional information:	Was born in Guyana, moved to England at the age of six, emigrated to Canada at nineteen, and moved to New York for MBA studies at age thirty-two; has traveled extensively in Africa, Asia, Europe, as well as in North America

Profile 3
Bambi Totts

Gender:	Female
Age:	23
Marital status:	Single
Religious affiliation:	No affiliation expressed
Family:	Lives at home with parents
Education:	B.A. in French
Languages:	Speaks French fluently; speaks some Spanish and Italian
Experience:	Joined BJP two years ago as a clerk in the Translation Department; has been promoted to a junior translation position
International experience:	None
Personality:	Cheerful, outgoing, and talkative; highly recommended by her superior
Hobbies:	Music, dancing, aerobics
Additional information:	Picks up foreign languages easily; has traveled throughout Canada and the United States; expresses interest in a foreign assignment as providing an opportunity to meet new people and experience different ways of life

Profile 4
Mohammed Smith

Gender:	Male
Age:	45
Marital status:	Married
Religious affiliation:	No affiliation expressed
Family:	Wife was born in Germany and moved to the United States when she was very young; she is currently employed as a social worker; three children—ages 23, 18, and 12; the eldest child is married, and the second has just entered college
Education:	B.S. in Engineering
Languages:	Speaks some German
Experience:	Joined BJP's Engineering Division ten years ago; prior to that, he worked as director of engineering for a small manufacturing company
International experience:	None
Personality:	Serious, reliable, energetic; those who work with him think highly of him
Hobbies:	Chess, classical music
Additional information:	German roots; has traveled in Europe on several vacations; owns a home in the country and devotes spare time to his home and family

Profile 5
Luis Alvarez

Gender:	Male
Age:	26
Marital status:	Single
Religious affiliation:	Nominally Roman Catholic
Family:	Lives alone
Education:	B.A. in Chemistry; MBA
Languages:	Speaks some Spanish and Russian
Experience:	Joined BJP's Research and Development Department two years ago
International experience:	None
Personality:	Works hard but is easygoing and well liked; enjoys meeting people of different ethnic backgrounds and is tolerant of different views
Hobbies:	Basketball
Additional information:	Describes himself as "fascinated by languages"—as a child, he would listen to foreigners and try to figure out what languages they were speaking; has made a point of learning as many languages as possible; not fluent in any foreign languages but is familiar with several; has traveled in the British Isles and has visited Mexico and Brazil; believes his tolerance for different views will serve him well in unfamiliar overseas environments

Profile 6
Katherine Wilson

Gender:	Female
Age:	38
Marital status:	Divorced
Religious affiliation:	No strong affiliation
Family:	Lives alone; devotes much of her free time to her elderly mother
Education:	Joint MBA/law degree
Languages:	Speaks no foreign languages but has often worked with interpreters
Experience:	Joined BJP's Legal Department seven years ago and has been promoted steadily within the department
International experience:	Has traveled extensively for the company and is familiar with overseas operations
Personality:	Reserved, strong, controlled personality; respected by colleagues and subordinates but does not socialize much, and they do not feel they know her well
Hobbies:	Tennis, reading
Additional information:	She is highly regarded by managers in foreign affiliates

Profile 7
Peter Schwartz

Gender:	Male
Age:	35
Marital status:	Married
Religious affiliation:	No affiliation expressed
Family:	Married to a financial analyst; two children, ages five and seven
Education:	B.S. in Accounting
Languages:	Speaks no foreign languages
Experience:	Has worked for BJP for fifteen years; started on a part-time basis when he was still in college
International experience:	None
Personality:	Hard worker; usually arrives at the office at 7:00 A.M. and stays late if there is work to be done
Hobbies:	Avid nature photographer; spends much of his outside time on this hobby and has had some photographs published
Additional information:	He and his wife have made a point of visiting different countries each year when vacationing, and they are enthusiastic about spending an extended period in a foreign location; they are concerned, however, about his wife's career and their children's education

Profile 8
Jean Bade

Gender:	Male
Age:	42
Marital status:	Married
Religious affiliation:	Practicing Catholic; religion described as playing a relatively minor role in his life
Family:	Wife is an elementary school teacher; one child, age 14
Education:	No college degree
Languages:	Speaks no foreign languages fluently
Experience:	Has worked for BJP for ten years; has risen through the company ranks to become vice president of Sales
International experience:	Has traveled extensively as a sales representative in Australia, Singapore, and Hong Kong
Personality:	Colleagues describe him alternately as "hot tempered" and "adaptive"; makes friends easily
Hobbies:	Coaches a little league baseball team
Additional information:	Gets along in foreign locations even when he does not speak the language—has a knack for picking up a few words and appropriate gestures that make his hosts comfortable

Profile 9
Richard Capwell

Gender:	Male
Age:	25
Marital status:	Engaged
Religious affiliation:	Muslim
Family:	Has an apartment in the city; parents, who he sees often; fiancée has just graduated from college and is seeking employment; she speaks several foreign languages
Education:	B.S. in Accounting
Languages:	Speaks no foreign languages
Experience:	Recently joined BJP after working for a large public accounting firm for three years; has had a great deal of responsibility early in his career and has performed well
International experience:	Organized and ran European biking tours during summers at college
Personality:	Described as relaxed and easygoing, yet produces at a very high level
Hobbies:	Sports
Additional information:	Father is Lebanese; mother is British; they live in the United States, where Richard was born; has not traveled much but describes himself as being culturally adaptable because of his mixed ethnicity; sees his fiancée's language ability as a plus in an overseas assignment

Profile 10
Karen Coombs

Gender:	Female
Age:	30
Marital status:	Married
Religious affiliation:	No religious affiliation expressed
Family:	Husband is high school teacher; no children
Education:	B.A. in Russian; MBA with a major in International Business
Languages:	Speaks Russian
Experience:	Joined the BJP Personnel Department as a specialist in international relations two years ago; previously worked with an international consulting company
International experience:	Has visited a variety of foreign locations for brief periods; has worked with foreign companies setting up operations in Canada and the United States
Personality:	Described as an enthusiastic, hard working, and dedicated employee
Hobbies:	Reading (science fiction and Russian novels), walking
Additional information:	Her parents are from Eastern Europe, but she has always lived in North America; she looks forward to the opportunity to spend an extended period overseas because she has enjoyed her previous visits to new countries

Project 5
PCN/HCN/TCN Choices

The purpose of this project is to decide on the appropriate nationality for managing a subsidiary in a particular location. The class will be divided into groups of four or five. Each group will be assigned two or three countries to consider. You have three broad choices: parent country nationals (PCNs), host country nationals (HCNs), and third country nationals (TCNs). You are asked to make a general assessment of which group(s) would be most appropriate for various management levels for your particular countries.

Your assessment should consider:

- host country regulations and laws;
- availability of potential managers;
- training of managers;
- acceptance of foreigners;
- cultural gaps;
- religious, racial, ethnic, or other biases; and
- headquarters control over policies and practices.

Based on this information, your group should decide whether HCNs, PCNs, or TCNs would be most appropriate for top, middle, and supervisory management in your assigned countries. A brief summary of your recommendations, and reasons for these recommendations, will be presented to the class orally and a written summary will be handed in to your instructor.

Project 6
Establishing a Subsidiary

This project gives students the opportunity to make decisions about organizing a subsidiary to fit into an existing organization. Student groups will be assigned a case with which to work (possibly one of the mini-cases in this book) and a country to consider. The company described in the case is establishing a new subsidiary in the country under consideration. Each group will decide on an appropriate structure for the subsidiary under different ownership conditions and recommend a preferred ownership option.

The three ownership possibilities are:

1. the subsidiary is wholly owned;
2. the subsidiary is a joint venture, where your company has a majority share; or
3. the subsidiary is a joint venture, where your company has a minority share.

Groups should consider the following when making their decisions:

- present structure of the organization;
- parent company policies towards subsidiaries;
- geographic location of the subsidiary; and
- cultural differences between the headquarters and the subsidiary.

Group reports should include the following in their discussions:

- overall relationships with headquarters and other subsidiaries;
- reporting relationships;
- degree of autonomy and decision-making authority;
- functional responsibilities; and
- functions and services provided by headquarters.

Project 7
Additional Exercises

The mini-cases can be used in a variety of additional exercises and projects; for example:

- developing a marketing program for a different country;
- creating a business plan for expansion to a particular location; or
- comparing investment opportunities in different countries.

The personal profiles can be used in a variety of additional exercises and projects as well; for example:

- designing a compensation package for an individual;
- developing a training program for an individual; or
- designing an overseas support system and career plan for an individual.

The instructor may ask students to suggest particular aspects of international business management that they would like to explore and then have the students design exercises for the class; for example:

- negotiating with the Russians, the Japanese, or the Chinese;
- developing a handbook for doing business in Latin America, North Africa or the Arab countries; or
- understanding the role of religion in international strategy.

The possibilities for additional exercises and projects are endless. I hope that those presented in this workbook will encourage users to develop additional ones to suit their particular needs. (If you develop new exercises that you find particularly valuable and would like to share them with me and others, I would be delighted if you would send them to me.)*

---

*My contact information is as follows:
Betty Jane Punnett
Department of Management Studies
University of the West Indies
Cave Hill
Barbados

Students may also be asked to identify a topic for an oral presentation or written paper. Following are some suggestions:

- current issues affecting international business
- the impact of the 9/11 terrorist attacks on the growth of international business
- changes in trading patterns over the past decade and reasons for these changes
- changes in foreign direct investment patterns over the past decade and reasons for these changes
- multidomestic versus global firms: advantages and disadvantages of different structures
- ownership: how much is appropriate?
- joint ventures: who makes a good partner?
- joint ventures: what contributes to success?
- Free Trade of the Americas: who wins? who loses?
- exports versus investment: a comparison of the advantages and disadvantages
- what makes a good international licensing agreement?
- what conditions are needed to franchise internationally?
- developments in the standardization of global accounting practices
- challenges in political risk assessment in today's environment
- marketing standardization: when and where it works
- managing international financial risk
- matching culture and negotiation tactics
- matching culture and leadership style
- motivating employees in developing countries
- managing culture shock
- how to prepare for and succeed in an international assignment
- communicating effectively when you do not speak the language
- the role of social responsibility in international management
- global corporate ethics: do they exist?
- paying the piper: how to manage when bribery is accepted practice

I have tried to cover a range of areas to stimulate your thinking, but there are so many more that you, as a student, may think of. The key is to identify a broad area of interest and then to frame a topic within that area that is fairly specific but allows for in-depth research.

In preparing a paper or presentation, a student's main concern is sometimes the mark that will be assigned, while the instructor's main concern is evaluating the degree of learning illustrated in the paper or presentation. Instructors may have marking schemes that reflect the particular content and focus of a particular course. However, certain factors are likely to be considered important in preparing any paper or presentation, and students who want good marks should include them:

Breadth of coverage: Has the student covered a variety of materials from a variety of sources (including texts, academic journals, magazines, current news, and the Internet)? Does the student demonstrate a well-rounded appreciation of the topic?

Depth of coverage: Has the student gone beyond a superficial examination of the topic? Has the student demonstrated a meaningful understanding of the topic?

Appropriateness of coverage: Are the materials used especially relevant to the topic under discussion? Does the student highlight special material to demonstrate appreciation and understanding of the topic?

Logic of presentation and arguments: Has the student been able to relate diverse arguments to one another? Has the student reached conclusions that are justified and well argued?

Style of presentation and writing: Is the paper or presentation easy to read or follow? Does it keep one's interest? Does it conform to required standards in terms of such factors as length, format, and references?

Case Studies

The following mini-cases are in the form of summary descriptions; these descriptions might have been prepared from information in the companies' annual reports and supplemented by interviews with managers and employees. They are brief but contain a good deal of information. The profiles include information on ownership, business, locations, world-wide sales, size, structure, management, training, communications and control, company strengths, company concerns, corporate strategy, and competition. This information gives you a basis for assessing the companies' strengths and weaknesses and their opportunities and challenges, and for making decisions in a realistic framework. Because the information is limited, you may find it necessary to make assumptions about the companies for certain decisions; be sure to make these assumptions explicit in your discussions.

Students as individuals, or in groups, should address the following questions:

1. What are the company's major strengths from an international perspective?
2. What are the company's major weaknesses from an international perspective?
3. What global opportunities can you identify for the company?
4. What challenges does the company face globally?
5. What changes, if any, would you suggest, with regard to: stated strategy, ownership policy, makeup of management, selection and training of management and employees, organizational structure, communications and control?

Case 1
Forms, Inc.

Forms, Inc. (FI) is a globally-owned company with shares sold on all of the major stock markets of the world. FI was founded in 1926 by a wealthy European family, which retains control of the company with the largest holding (10 percent). Almost all subsidiaries are wholly owned, and FI prefers 100 percent ownership in foreign operations. Joint ventures have been established, where required locally, when the location has been seen as strategically important to FI. In these situations, FI prefers local partners who do not want to be actively involved in decision making. FI produces and markets business forms and computer software worldwide. Business forms represent 78 percent of sales; software, 20 percent; and the final 2 percent is provided by a variety of related mechanical products (e.g., storage racks and other forms-related equipment). FI headquarters are in Belgium, although only 3 percent of sales are generated there. The company has sales offices in over 100 countries and production operations in fifteen.

Sales. Approximately US$2 billion in 1998: 40 percent of sales are in Europe, 10 percent in Africa, 15 percent in the Middle East, 5 percent in the former Communist bloc, 10 percent in Japan and the Pacific Rim, 10 percent in Latin America and the Caribbean, and 10 percent in Canada and the United States.

Size. Approximately 25,000 employees worldwide; over 600 sales offices.

Structure. The company is organized around two mainstreams of activity: (1) production and customer service, and (2) marketing and sales. These are seen by top management as equally important aspects of the organization. Both production and sales are organized regionally; however, the regions are not necessarily contiguous. Each center is operated as a profit center with regional coordinating committees serving as liaisons between them.

Regional Production Centers. Regional production centers have been identified on the basis of efficiency and integration of operations. Five production center regions have been established: (1) the United States and South and Central America, (2) Western Europe, (3) Southern Europe, (4) the Middle East and Africa, and (5) the Far East.
   Production facilities are located in the following countries:

Area 1: United States, Mexico, Barbados, Brazil
Area 2: Belgium, France, Switzerland
Area 3: Greece, Italy, Spain
Area 4: Nigeria, Zambia, Saudi Arabia
Area 5: Australia, Malaysia

Regional Sales Centers. Regional sales centers have been identified on the basis of local variation in customer needs and buying habits. Eight sales center regions have been established: (1) the United States and Canada, (2) South America, (3) Central America and the Caribbean, (4) the European Union, (5) former Communist bloc countries, (6) Japan, (7) South Africa, and (8) Africa (except South Africa).

Sales facilities are located in the following countries:

Area 1: three in Canada and five in the United States
Area 2: one in each—Argentina, Brazil, Chile
Area 3: one in each—Barbados, Costa Rica
Area 4: one in each—Belgium, France, the UK
Area 5: one in Russia
Area 6: two in Japan
Area 7: one in South Africa
Area 8: one in each—Kenya, Nigeria, the United Arab Emirates

Coordinating Committees. Coordinating committees have been established to overcome some of the difficulties presented by the different makeup of the two types of regional centers; coordinating committees are located in the following regions: (1) the Americas, (2) Europe, (3) the Middle East and Africa, and (4) the Far East.

Management. All of the top managers are European, and most of the salespeople are also European. Production management and personnel are mostly local residents once operations are established, but there is always one "home office" representative. This representative is expected to oversee operations and quality control and provide a communication link between the subsidiary and the home office. These home office representatives have extensive international experience as they generally do not spend more than three years in one location.

Training. Salespeople receive extensive training not only technically, but also culturally. Cultural training includes films and lectures on the host culture, intensive language instruction, and interaction with host nationals and foreigners who have lived in the host country. Salespeople generally stay in one region for several years and work with their replacements for several months before leaving. Management receives similar training for overseas posts.

Communications and Control. Top managers believe in personal communications and visit subsidiaries regularly. Their philosophy is that you have to know your people personally if you expect them to work hard. In addition, regional meetings are held regularly, and subsidiary managers visit the home office once a year. Social functions are also held regularly to celebrate local achievements. Personal interaction and supervision constitutes a large part of the control system—ensuring that things are done the FI way. There is also a formal system of written reports, which are sent to the home office by the subsidiary management on a weekly, biweekly, and monthly basis.

Company Strengths. The company has been very successful; this can be attributed to its product innovation, as well as to efficient manufacturing. Efficiency has been achieved through standardized production processes. Manufacturing operations are identical wherever they are located. The buildings are built to the same specifications; the layout and the machinery are the same. Thus, an operator from Spain could be flown to Barbados and immediately find his or her way around the factory.

Product innovation has been achieved through localization, that is, through responsiveness to local needs, customs, and so on. Sales and marketing personnel provide customized approaches for their customers; they monitor changing needs in different locations and respond to them. However, they also are trained to look for similarities in various locations and to capitalize on them to increase the use of standard forms.

Company Concerns. "Trade-offs" best summarize the company's concerns. The two arms of the company—production and sales—are in conflict regarding short-term objectives. In addition, local management is in conflict with headquarters over objectives, reports, and evaluations. Communication throughout the organization is difficult, and overseas personnel feel out of touch with the organization as a whole. The organizational structure is complex and results in delays as coordinating committees travel from one location to another, attempting to integrate production and sales. These delays have resulted in directives from top management in Belgium, which add to intra-company conflicts.

Corporate Strategy. Rapid expansion is planned for the next five years. Top management believes it can increase sales dramatically in the Pacific Rim, Latin America, and North America. This will require an expanded sales force in these locations, as well as increased production facilities. Top management is currently examining the operating and profit potential in the former Communist countries.

Competition. Globally there are two other firms that produce and sell business forms, computer software, and related items throughout the world: one is Canadian; the other, British. At the local level, there are small printing companies in virtually every country offering some products similar to FI's.

Case 2

Black Beauty Corp.

Black Beauty Corp. (BBC) is controlled by the Carter family who own 51 percent of outstanding shares; 20 percent is owned by management and employees; the balance is traded publicly on the New York Stock Exchange. The Carter family established the company in 1955 in Detroit as a small, family-run operation. Growth in sales during the 1960s led to a public offering of shares in 1968, and in 1970, an employee-ownership program was initiated.

BBC produces and sells cosmetics for black consumers. The business began in the 1950s when Mrs. Carter found it impossible to obtain cosmetics suitable for her own dark complexion. She experimented with a variety of ingredients and developed several products that she and her friends found acceptable. From this small beginning, BBC has grown to be one of the largest suppliers in the world of cosmetics for black consumers.

BBC's headquarters are in Detroit, but it operates decentralized production facilities throughout the United States. Seventy-five percent of sales are in the United States, with the majority in the South and Northeast. In 1991, BBC entered the international market by establishing a plant in Jamaica to serve Caribbean countries; in 1992, BBC opened a second overseas production facility in Zimbabwe to explore the African market; and in 1994, BBC opened a third foreign facility in England to serve British and European locations. Currently, 10 percent of its sales is to the Caribbean, half of this supplied by products produced domestically in Jamaica; 5 percent of its sales is to the African market, supplied entirely from the Zimbabwe facility; and 10 percent of sales is to Britain and Europe, supplied entirely from the British facility.

Sales. Total sales for 2000 were US$40 million. Sales rose dramatically during the 1960s at close to 15 percent a year. During the 1970s, they continued to rise, but growth slowed to about 5 percent a year. In the 1990s growth in the U.S. market has stopped, and there even appears to have been a declining trend.

Structure. The company is organized into geographic divisions in the United States; an international division is responsible for all foreign operations, including exports. Within the United States, each division is a profit center responsible for sales and production of all products. These divisions enjoy a fair amount of autonomy, with overall strategy determined by the head office. All of the foreign subsidiaries report to the vice president of International Operations, an American.

Profitability. U.S. profits have declined from a high of 30 percent return on equity in 1970 to a low of 1.6 percent in 2000. Overseas operations have consistently lost money. The Jamaican facility showed small profits in its third and fourth years of operation but is now operating at a loss. This is attributed to low quality levels and supply inconsistencies due to strikes that have resulted in customers ordering directly from U.S. suppliers. The Zimbabwean operation has experienced many difficulties, and projected sales have never materialized. The British operation has lost money but appears to have turned the corner and is expected to be profitable in the coming year.

Management. The top managers are all citizens of the United States; all are African American. Foreign production facilities are staffed by a mixture of Americans and locals. Top management would like to increase the percentage of locals in management positions in subsidiaries but has had difficulty finding qualified locals in Jamaica and Zimbabwe. Qualified locals in Britain are generally white, and this is felt to conflict with BBC's overall image as a "black company." Managers have been sent from the United States to establish overseas operations and train local managers. Initially, the intention was that they should remain for a maximum of three years, but in all cases, the U.S. managers have remained and are still operating the facilities on a day-to-day basis.

Corporate Strategy. The company produces a wide range of well-known products of high quality; these products are unique in many parts of the world. The company spends a competitive percentage (2 percent) of its sales dollar on research and development and a substantial percentage (15 percent) on advertising and promotion. The company's image as a "black company" is believed to be important to its customers as well.

Company Concerns. BBC is losing market share, and the total U.S. market is declining; it appears that many African-American consumers are using products designed primarily for white consumers and find these satisfactory. Overseas operations have not filled the gap created by a declining U.S. market, as BBC had hoped.

Corporate Strategy. BBC intends to expand its foreign markets but is still in the process of formulating an operational policy to achieve this objective. The company is examining the possibility of increasing its target market to include other nonwhite races. There appears to be substantial potential in the Pacific Rim countries.

Case 3

Beverages Inc. International

Beverages Inc. International (BII) is a holding company with its head office in New York and subsidiaries in ten countries. The ownership is difficult to describe: its principal shareholders, accounting for 30 percent of ownership, are two other large multinational companies—one based in the United States and one in France; the balance of shares in the holding company are widely owned. Ownership in subsidiaries ranges from 100 percent ownership to 50-50 joint ventures to minority ownership, depending on the situation and particular products to be manufactured or sold. The company believes that each foreign subsidiary should be approached as a new project and structured according to the needs of the specific situation.

Business. BII's main business is distilling; it is the world's largest producer of distilled spirits. In addition, it produces an extensive line of wines. BII's major products are recognized worldwide and include products that are of high quality and expensive, as well as those that are moderately priced. In addition to its major business as a distiller and wine producer, BII comprises various unrelated businesses such as hardware retailing, fashion boutiques, and computer software. All of these businesses contribute to a profitable consolidated income statement, but distilling remains its major business.

Structure. The company has a global regional structure for its distilling business. Production and sales are organized into geographic groups, each reporting to its own regional vice president, located in New York. These groups correspond to sales as follows: United States and Canada, the European Union, and other foreign operations. Although the company considers itself global and theoretically considers all markets important, the dominance of its domestic market means that this tends to dominate top-management thinking.

Locations. The company has distilling operations in ten of the industrialized countries of the world (the United States, Canada, Britain, France, Germany, Australia, New Zealand, Japan, Sweden, and Denmark) and sells its products throughout the world. The company produces and sells identical products worldwide, but certain product lines are more popular in certain locations.

Sales. Sales in 2002 totaled US$3 billion worldwide. Sales in the United States account for 55 percent of total; sales to Canada, 10 percent; sales in the European Union, 20 percent; and the rest of the world, 15 percent. The company employs about 15,000 people worldwide. New products are first developed for the U.S. market then test marketed in other locations once accepted in the home market.

Management. Top management is a mix of Americans, Canadians, and Europeans. The company has made a specific effort to diversify the makeup of its board of directors, as well as its executives. Management in subsidiaries is also generally mixed, the majority being ocal, then some Americans, and then others from third countries. BII's motto in this regard s "the best person for the job regardless of nationality." Despite efforts to "globalize" management's thinking, middle management still thinks of the United States as "home" and as its major market; and upper management tends to view foreign assignments as possibly detracting from, or prohibiting, career advancement. In addition, the failure rate of foreign assignees (about 15 percent of foreign assignments become defined as "failures") has been a concern to the company.

Training. American personnel who are going abroad participate in a two-week training program prior to leaving the home country. This program focuses on cultural differences and ways of doing business. Proposed local managers of foreign operations spend a two-week period in a U.S. distilling facility and two weeks at the head office in New York prior to undertaking management responsibilities. It is believed that this helps them understand the need for following the company's prescribed policies and procedures.

Communications and Control. Both production and marketing are standardized globally. Although some production and marketing adaptations are made for local conditions, the same products are made worldwide and marketed with the same message. Consequently, production and marketing decisions are made almost entirely at the head office. These decisions are communicated to the divisions in writing; foreign subsidiaries, as well as U.S. operations, follow through on them, providing periodic reports on progress. The head office provides specific goals, objectives, policies, and procedures, but it is then left up to local management to decide how best to achieve goals and objectives and implement policies and procedures.

Company Strengths. The company's size and worldwide recognition in the distilling industry are its basic strengths. Its accumulated international experience serves as a basis for further international expansion. Diversification into unrelated businesses has served to cushion the company from negative shocks to the distillery business.

Company Concerns. The company's focus remains domestic in spite of efforts to globalize. The domestic market is seen as a mature market, while many overseas markets are growth markets; the company must capitalize on these now or lose international market share to competitors. The failure rate of expatriate managers is also a concern; this may be related to the company's lack of global view.

Corporate Strategy. BII intends to capitalize on its strengths to expand globally. It intends to push its quality image with a global advertising program and to back this up with increased foreign production. Currently, BII is examining the feasibility of establishing production facilities in a wide variety of locations throughout the world.

Competition. There are several large global companies in the distilling business and many small local companies; thus, BII faces a wide variety of competition. The large, global companies are recognized worldwide, just as BII is; the small, local companies generally enjoy local government protection. Alcoholic beverages have traditionally been subject to high import tariffs and duties, as well as high local taxes; thus, local competitors can prove to be serious competition.

Case 4
International Products, Ltd.

Ownership. A large multinational company, International Products Ltd. (IPL) has its head-quarters in New York City. IPL has a wide variety of affiliations with other companies in other countries as well as a number of subsidiaries. Top management at headquarters is almost entirely American.

IPL recently established a majority-owned subsidiary—Offshore Products—in a small developing country. The company owns 60 percent of the subsidiary; the other 40 percent is owned by a wealthy local businessman.

Business. Offshore Products assembles electronic components, which it sells to other sub-sidiaries of IPL; assembly materials are provided by headquarters and billed to Offshore Products. IPI also provides Offshore Products with machinery and supplies that are not available locally, as well as management assistance.

Management. Management at Offshore Products consists of three locals and two Ameri-cans. The expectation is that the two Americans will remain until they are confident that the local managers are capable of running operations on their own. It was initially hoped that the Americans would be there for one year, but after a year of operations they have indicated that they believe they will have to remain for a second year. The local partner is not involved in the day-to-day operations of Offshore Products but provides advice and assistance on local matters when requested.

Company Concerns. Offshore Products has completed its first year of operations and its performance is being reviewed by a top management group in New York. Costs have been substantially higher than anticipated, and Offshore Products is losing money (see Exhibit 8). The headquarters management group must consider:

1. the performance of the U.S. managers at Offshore Products;
2. the performance of the local managers at Offshore Products; and
3. evaluation of overall operations.

The loss incurred by Offshore Products is small relative to IPL's other operations. Never-theless, it is unexpected and raises a number of issues that headquarters must resolve. IPL must decide how, and indeed if, operations at Offshore Products should continue. The issue is complicated by the fact that there was a change in government in the country six months ago, and IPL is unsure of its relationship with the new government. Further, there are ru-mors of a forthcoming devaluation of the country's currency.

Exhibit 8

Subsidiary Performance

	Actual	Projected
Net sales	$1,200,000	$1,000,000
Less:		
Materials	540,000	400,000
Direct labor	300,000	200,000
Import duties[a]	90,000	—
Depreciation	50,000	50,000
	980,000	650,000
Gross profit	220,000	350,000
Administrative expenses:		
Management salaries and expenses	230,000	200,000
Staff expenses[b]	100,000	75,000
Other expenses	100,000	75,000
	430,000	350,000
Net loss	(210,000)	—

[a]A request is being considered by the government for a refund of import duties.

[b]The local partner received a $50,000 consultation fee; the balance was for services from headquarters.

Case 5

Bata Shoe Organization

Company Philosophy. A story is told that following World War II, two footwear companies sent representatives to assess the African markets. One returned and said that there was no market because the people did not wear shoes. The other returned and said that the market was huge because the people did not wear shoes. The second representative worked for the Bata Shoe Organization (BSO). This story's approach to worldwide opportunities and the attitude that exemplifies BSO has resulted in the firm becoming the largest manufacturer and marketer of footwear in the world.

Ownership. BSO was started as a family business in the late 1800s in Czechoslovakia. It remains a family business, with the founder's grandson at its helm as chief executive officer. The firm's headquarters is now in Toronto, Canada, but 95 percent of its business is outside of Canada. BSO operates in more than 100 countries worldwide.

Corporate Structure. The firm describes itself as a "multidomestic"; that is, a firm with subsidiaries operating as largely autonomous entities. BSO's corporate brochure describes the firm as "an international organization of companies rooted in their communities and essentially 'national' in spirit." BSO believes its first allegiance is to the community and countries where it does business. Subsidiaries operate as local companies and rely largely on local markets, local suppliers, and local staff. Interestingly, BSO has the reputation of being considered a local company almost everywhere it operates; in parts of Africa *bata* is a local word for shoes. This local image may be partly due to the fact that the name *bata* is not easily associated with any particular nationality.

Company Strengths. In contrast to BSO's multidomestic image, a policy of standardization appears to be one of the company's competitive strengths. Factories and stores are built and maintained to similar specifications around the world. Employees worldwide have access to the same management, technical, and training opportunities. Universal policies govern all the subsidiaries. This global standardization and control is possible because BSO establishes wholly-owned subsidiaries wherever possible (85 percent of subsidiaries are wholly owned).

Training. This mix of decentralization and global standardization is achieved partly through a training program that affects all BSO employees throughout their careers. BSO draws on the diversity represented by its worldwide presence while ensuring congruity among operations—for example, by bringing marketing managers from around the world together in Toronto to share their individual ideas and experiences and to develop new approaches to take back to their local operations.

Training at BSO takes place at all levels of the organization. There are programs for top management, middle management, supervisors, and operators, as well as training programs

148

for trainers. This is stressed throughout the organization, and there seems to be a genuine belief that proper training results in tangible benefits for both the organization and its people. These include higher productivity, lower absenteeism, improved industrial relations, and increased employee satisfaction.

A major challenge at BSO is the development of training programs that are culturally sensitive and can travel throughout the world. To achieve this combination, BSO has adopted the following approach:

- Upper-level management at headquarters in Toronto develops an agenda of general issues that they believe affect all members of a particular group (say supervisors), no matter where they are located. This agenda includes such issues as motivation, discipline, assigning work, communication, and so on. An overview, which describes the concept behind each issue, is then prepared.
- Individuals in various countries and regions then meet to discuss the issues identified. These groups consider various situations and identify possible ways of reacting to these situations. Out of this discussion, a culture-specific "good management" solution is defined. These discussions and solutions serve as the basis for training programs in the varied locations.

Company Strategy. BSO's particular mix of multidomestic and global standardization appears to have worked well. The firm continues to grow and be successful. Yet, there appear to be potential advantages to changing parts of the mix. Two possibilities are under consideration: (1) the firm could potentially benefit from economies of scale if its operations were more globally integrated; and (2) it could potentially benefit from local expertise and financing if it were more open to alternative ownership arrangements.

About the Author

Betty Jane Punnett, a native of St. Vincent and the Grenadines, is professor of international business at the Cave Hill Campus of the University of the West Indies. She taught at the University of Windsor for fifteen years and has lived and worked in the Caribbean, Canada, Europe, Asia, and the United States. Her major research interest is culture and management, and she is currently working on several research projects in this field. She holds a PhD in international business from New York University, an MBA from Marist College, and a BA from McGill University. Her latest book, *International Perspectives on Organizational Behavior and Human Resource Management,* was published by M.E. Sharpe in 2004.